HE HAS MADE ME GLAD

ENJOYING GOD'S GOODNESS

WITH RECKLESS ABANDON

BEN PATTERSON

InterVarsity Press
Downers Grove, Illinois

InterVarsity Press
P.O. Box 1400, Downers Grove, IL 60515-1426
World Wide Web: www.ivpress.com
E-mail: mail@ivpress.com

InterVarsity Press® is the book-publishing division of InterVarsity Christian Fellowship/USA®, a student movement active on campus at hundreds of universities, colleges and schools of nursing in the United States of America, and a member movement of the International Fellowship of Evangelical Students. For information about local and regional activities, write Public Relations Dept., InterVarsity Christian Fellowship/USA, 6400 Schroeder Rd., P.O. Box 7895, Madison, WI 53707-7895, or visit the IVCF website at <www.intervarsity.org>.

All Scripture quotations, unless otherwise indicated, are taken from the Holy Bible, New International Version®. NIV®. Copyright ©1973, 1978, 1984 by International Bible Society. Used by permission of Zondervan Publishing House. All rights reserved.

Design: Cindy Kiple

Images: Charles Mason/Getty Images

ISBN 0-8308-1743-3

Printed in the United States of America ∞

Library of Congress Cataloging-in-Publication Data

Patterson, Ben, 1942-
  He has made me glad: enjoying God's goodness with reckless
abandon
  / Ben Patterson.
    p. cm.
  Includes bibliographical references.
  ISBN 0-8308-1743-3 (pbk.: alk. paper)
  1. Joy—Religious aspects—Christianity. 2. Grace (Theology) 3.
God—Goodness. 4. Christian life. I. Title
  BV4647.J68P38 2005
  248.4—dc22

                                   2004025503

P	18	17	16	15	14	13	12	11	10	9	8	7	6	5	4	3	2	1
Y	18	17	16	15	14	13	12	11	10	09	08	07	06	05				

To the good people of

The Presbyterian Church of New Providence, New Jersey,

where the seeds for this book were

planted in hard soil and watered with tears.

They have brought a harvest of joy.

Thank you!

Charis. Eucharistia. Chara.

"Those who sow in tears
will reap with songs of joy."
PSALM 126:5

CONTENTS

INTRODUCTION

We Are Far Too Easily Pleased

*We are half-hearted creatures, fooling about with
drink and sex and ambition when infinite joy is offered us.*

C. S. LEWIS

W hat's your heart's desire? A poll conducted by the George Barna
organization a few years ago discovered that the number one desire of
most Americans was to be thinner. Number two was to be richer. If the
pollsters had called you, what would you have listed as your heart's desire? Maybe it's to have a fulfilling vocation or to be rich and famous. Or
maybe you simply want to be happy. What do you think God thinks of
your heart's desire? Do you want too much or too little?

In an old *Peanuts* cartoon Lucy asks Charlie Brown what his goal in
life is. He pauses, thinks about the question for a few frames and answers, without blinking, "To be outrageously happy."[1] Apparently the
cartoonist, Charles Schulz, thought that was funny, that outrageous happiness was an outrageous expectation. Maybe God thinks so too.

Then again, maybe he doesn't. C. S. Lewis was of the opposite opinion:

> If we consider the unblushing promises of reward and the stagger-
> ing nature of the rewards promised in the Gospels, it would seem
> that our Lord finds our desires not too strong, but too weak. We
> are half-hearted creatures, fooling about with drink and sex and

ambition when infinite joy is offered us, like an ignorant child who wants to go on making mud pies in a slum because he cannot imagine what is meant by the offer of a holiday at the sea. We are far too easily pleased.[2]

Infinite joy. Now that's a prospect. Could that actually be what God is offering us? And is it true that we want not too much, but too little? I intend to show that it is. That is the burden of this book.

FRANTIC ENERGY AND VIRTUAL JOYS

Although writing about God's joy is an easy burden and a delight to carry, it makes me feel tongue-tied, like the first time I saw the Pacific Ocean. It had been described to me many times; I had read about it and seen pictures of it. As we neared the water, I caught glimpses between the houses along the beach. Then we came up over a rise and there it was—huge, mysterious, almost frightening. I felt as though it might swallow me up. Nothing I had been told could prepare me for the experience. Infinite joy is like that. G. K. Chesterton believed its "frantic energy . . . would knock us down like a drunken farce," that "the laughter of the heavens is too loud for us to hear."[3]

It takes a lot of imagination to get one's mind around the idea of infinite joy. See if this helps: In May 1982 a solar flare shot out from the sun and was so huge that scientific instruments couldn't measure it. Scientists do know that in its twenty-minute existence the flare released more energy than all the energy, both natural and manufactured, produced on earth in one year.[4] Anyone within a million miles of that explosion would have been incinerated. Now, can you imagine a love that is to human love what that explosion was to a flashlight? Or a joy whose richness and intensity blaze forth with such dazzling power that it makes our joy seem like a feeble match flame? Such is the glory of God's character, what Kierkegaard called the infinite qualitative distance between God and us.

Holy, infinite joy: to experience it fully in our present state would shatter our fragile nervous systems. We must be spiritually transformed in order to receive it completely. So although I've read about joy, thought and talked about it, I've still experienced it only a little. But perhaps I know enough to whet your appetite. Think of this book as a kind of hors d'oeuvre. There are so many joy counterfeits in the world that it's easy to be duped. I call these "virtual joys," experiences that give the sensation of joy without the reality. Drink, sex and ambition are just a few. In religious circles we often think we're feeling joy when we bubble over with shrill, vacuous expressions that turn up the volume and turn off the mind. In our youth-obsessed culture the diversions we use to avoid facing the reality of death are sometimes labeled joy. Pascal wrote, "Being unable to cure death, wretchedness and ignorance, men have decided, in order to be happy, not to think about such things."[5] But if joy is anything, it is the strength to think about such things, to look directly at the cold realities of life, say "Nevertheless!" and be joyful.

THE MARVELOUS AND IMPOSSIBLE

I cry almost every time I talk about joy. Why does joy involve tears? I think it's because, as Frederick Buechner suggests, "The marvelous and impossible thing truly happens."[6] Tears well up from that deep place where guilt and grace, human misery and divine love meet. Joy springs from the realization that things need not have been so good, in fact should not have been, but are. The inevitable is overtaken by the unforeseeable, mercy triumphs over judgment, and joy breaks in, "beyond the walls of the world, poignant as grief."[7] Tears of grief and tears of joy flow from very nearly the same place, and "those who sow in tears / will reap with songs of joy" (Psalm 126:5). Tears are a small price to pay for something like infinite joy, wouldn't you say?

The greatest enemy of joy is to not know what we're missing. In an old Hasidic tale Bontscha the Silent was passed over, forgotten, oppressed and denied. He withdrew from all desire, all hope. Expecting nothing, he had come to want nothing. For Bontscha there were no highs, lows, blacks or whites—only the gray numbness of resignation. When his body finally died, he found himself standing in the court of heaven, before the throne of the Almighty. God looked tenderly at

Bontscha and said, "My son, all your joyless life you had nothing. You lived without hope. But now, here in my presence, there is the fullness of joy, eternal pleasures at my right hand. Only ask, and you shall receive."

The shrunken little soul's eyes squinted as he pondered the offer. "Anything at all?" he asked.

"Yes," said the Almighty, "anything you want."

After a long pause, Bontscha said to the Almighty, "I would like a freshly baked roll, with real butter."

And heaven wept.

The great tragedy of Bontscha's life was not what he had been denied, but what he had ceased to desire. God had been reduced to the size of his longings. He had become far too easily pleased.[8]

Charles Spurgeon once prayed that God would send his congregation a season of "holy disorder." He wanted the worthless and lesser things to be shaken up and swept away so the deck could be cleared for God's fresh blessings. A similar prayer would be in order at the beginning of a book on joy, perhaps one like Augustine prayed:

> And how shall I call upon my God, my God and Lord, since when I call for Him, I shall be calling Him to myself? and what room is there within me, whither my God can come into me? Whither can God come into me, God who made heaven and earth? Is there, indeed, O Lord my God, aught in me that can contain Thee?[9]

The answer is no, nothing in us can contain him. Something radical must happen to us for God to come in. God must make room for God. He may have to sweep some things aside, and it may be messy, even painful to be expanded in our desires and capacities. But remember, he's making room for his joy. So we pray come, Holy Spirit, holy disorder.

PART ONE

THE CASE FOR JOY

Gratitude follows grace like

thunder lightning.

KARL BARTH

❧ 1 ❧

INEXPRESSIBLE AND
GLORIOUS JOY

*Though you have not seen him, you love him;
and even though you do not see him now, you believe in him
and are filled with an inexpressible and glorious joy,
for you are receiving the goal of your faith,
the salvation of your souls.*

1 PETER 1:8-9

*S*unday dinner at my grandma's house was always a memorable event. Food appeared on the massive oak table like royalty. King Roast Beef sat at one end of the table, Queen Mashed Potatoes reigned at the other end with Sir Gravy at her side, and the rest of the court surrounded them in splendor: fresh garden corn and tomatoes, home-baked bread, scallions and green peas, raspberry jam, ice cold milk and tea. Out of sight but giving off a delicious scent, the hot apple pie waited in state to be unveiled at the end.

Sunday dinner at Grandma's house was an occasion of reverence and joy.

The most memorable of these meals occurred when I was about eight years old. Since I especially loved the mashed potatoes and gravy, I always tried to position myself near them. On this particular day I sat with the vatlike bowl of potatoes right in front of my face, almost exactly at

eye level. Steam rose from the mountain of spuds, butter ran in rivers
down its canyons. As people gathered around the table, I pondered how
I would distribute the gravy. Should I build a little potato castle in the
middle, with a moat for the gravy around it? Or should I make a giant
lake in the middle? I decided on the lake.

When everyone was seated, Grandpa asked Uncle Albert to pray.
That's not his name, but I'll use the alias to . . . well, you'll see why. Uncle
Albert was an odd man from a part of the family that some of us were a
little uncomfortable with. I don't remember which church they went to,
but I once heard that they were "holy rollers." I didn't know what that
phrase meant, but since it was whispered I was reluctant to ask. I found
out when he started to give thanks. Albert prayed with great feeling and
volume. He was truly grateful for the food. So was I. But he was grateful
in detail. He thanked God for the scallions and the peas and the beef. He
rhapsodized over the plates and forks and knives. He sang of Grandma
and the "hands that prepared" the food. He extolled the name of God for
his wonderful generosity. He wept and clapped his hands for joy. I began
to notice the steam wasn't rising as high on the mashed potatoes. My
heart sank as his rose, and the potatoes grew cold.

I was disgusted when he finished and resentful for years afterward, but
the seed of a new idea was planted: You feel joy when you are grateful for
the grace that has been given you. Indeed, if we could ever take to heart
the goodness and generosity of God—really perceive its height, depth,
width and length (Ephesians 3:14-21)—we might act just like my Uncle
Albert. If our gratitude could perfectly correspond to the grace that is
given us, then no amount of thanksgiving and joy could be excessive.

THE TWIN CHILDREN OF GRACE

Gratitude and joy are the twin children of grace, organically joined both
theologically and spiritually. In Greek they are even related linguistically:
the words for grace, gratitude and joy all have the same root, *char,* a noun
that refers to health and well-being. "Grace" is *charis,* "gratitude" is *eucharistia,* and "joy" is *chara.*

What is merely a linguistic relationship in Greek is a burning reality in the kingdom of God. Grace is God's mercy, his unmerited favor. It is what Frederick Buechner calls the "crucial eccentricity" of the Christian faith, the unique and wonderfully odd thing God does to forgive sinners: he doesn't give them the bad things they deserve but the incredibly good things they don't deserve.[1] The great gospel mystery is not that bad things sometimes happen to good people, but that such a good thing has happened to bad people. The guilty and broken have discovered that "while we were still sinners, Christ died for us" (Romans 5:8). What else can we be but grateful? "How can anything more or different be asked of man?" asks Karl Barth. "The only answer to charis is eucharistia. . . . Grace and gratitude belong together like heaven and earth. Grace evokes gratitude like the voice of an echo. Gratitude follows grace like thunder lightning."[2]

And as gratitude follows grace, so joy follows gratitude, for joy is what we feel when we're hugely grateful. The pattern runs throughout Scripture: God does something wonderful and the people praise him joyfully. What else could they do—praise him somberly? Genuine gratitude must necessarily be joyful. The greater the grace, the greater the gratitude; the greater the gratitude, the greater the joy.

Psalm 95, for instance, begins with a call to be grateful and joyful in a big way:

Come, let us sing for joy to the LORD;
    let us shout aloud to the Rock of our salvation.
Let us come before him with thanksgiving
    and extol him with music and song. (Psalm 95:1-2)

Why such exuberance? Because God is super-outstanding, that's why.

For the LORD is the great God,
    the great King above all gods.
In his hand are the depths of the earth,
    and the mountain peaks belong to him.
The sea is his, for he made it,
    and his hands formed the dry land. (Psalm 95:3-5)

God's creative power is reason enough to be grateful and joyful. But there is more: not only is God beyond impressive in what he made, but he has taken a special liking to us. He is intimately involved in our well-being:

> For he is our God
>> and we are the people of his pasture,
>> the flock under his care. (Psalm 95:7)

The joy of genuine gratitude follows grace like thunder follows lightning.

Psalm 16 oozes with joy; its essence is compressed into the last verse:

> You have made known to me the path of life;
>> you fill me with joy in your presence,
>> with eternal pleasures at your right hand. (Psalm 16:11)

It's all there. The grace is the path of life, the exquisite presence of God, and eternal life. The gratitude and joy, like echoes in a canyon, are a result of the eternal pleasures we find at God's right hand.

These are but two examples from the book of Psalms, which is largely a libretto of joy and praise. This book, the largest in the Bible, begins with a description of the things that make for happiness—"delight . . . in the law of the LORD" (Psalm 1:2)—and ends with, "Let everything that has breath praise the LORD" (Psalm 150:6). Next to Genesis and Revelation, the Psalms are the easiest book to find. They sit, significantly I think, right at the center of the Bible—just like the gospel message.

MEGA-JOY FOR MEGA-FEAR

Since the same God comes to us in Jesus Christ, we can expect the same joyful pattern in the events surrounding his birth—only more so. When Mary, miraculously pregnant with Jesus, went to visit Elizabeth, who was pregnant with John, Elizabeth's infant got very active. Elizabeth exclaimed to Mary, "As soon as the sound of your greeting reached my ears, the baby in my womb leaped for joy" (Luke 1:44).

Now, mothers are accustomed to their babies twitching and kicking in the womb—sometimes they're convinced they've got a future Olympic medalist in there. Few, however, seriously connect emotions to the prenatal gymnastics. But Elizabeth knew, with intuitive theological accuracy, exactly what her baby was feeling. That's what happens when people see Jesus for who he is: spontaneous joy, even in the unborn.

The shepherds, on the other hand, needed a little help with their joy. Soon after Jesus was born in Bethlehem, an angel appeared in their camp to announce the happy event. For some reason, whenever people in the Bible meet angels, they don't feel touched or special. Shattered is more like it. The English for the shepherds' reaction is, "They were terrified." The Greek is, almost literally, they were "mega-afraid." The angel said, "Do not be afraid. I bring you good news of great joy that will be for all the people" (Luke 2:10). The great joy the angel speaks of is "mega-joy." In other words, the shepherds' mega-fear would be replaced by mega-joy when they saw Jesus.

Jesus taught that joy is one of the hallmarks of his kingdom. His mission statement was, "I have come that they may have life, and have it to the full" (John 10:10). What is fullness of life if not joyful? He also said, "I have told you this so that my joy may be in you and that your joy may be complete" (John 15:11). When people discover this, Jesus said, they are like a man who found treasure in a field and "hid it again, and then in his joy went and sold all he had and bought that field" (Matthew 13:44).

Jesus also taught about joy in his encounters with two women. The first story, found in Luke 7:36-50, is about a woman of sexually immoral repute who committed an act of gross social impropriety: she walked alone into an all-male luncheon. In attendance were respected city fathers hosted by a Pharisee named Simon. When the men spotted her in the doorway, the room turned deathly silent. Everyone wondered whom she knew in the room. The only sound was that of her bare feet padding across the stone floor. They were relieved when she stopped beside Jesus. Weeping, she knelt down at his feet and let her tears fall. Simon had conspicuously not extended the basic courtesy of having Jesus' feet washed, so her tears did the job. Little rivulets of mud ran down the sides of his feet as she undid her long black hair and used it to wipe them clean. Then, with an intimacy that almost made the men blush, she broke open a vial of expensive, fragrant ointment and massaged its contents into Jesus' feet.

Meanwhile, Simon's thoughts were ugly: *If he were who he says he is, he'd know what she is and he wouldn't let a woman like that touch him. But he probably knows all too well what she is.*

Jesus responded to Simon's thoughts: "I tell you, her sins—and they are many—have been forgiven, so she has shown me much love. But a person who is forgiven little shows only little love" (Luke 7:47 NLT). In other words, her actions corresponded perfectly to the grace given her. Simon's clearly didn't. Do ours? Can any of us truthfully say we have been forgiven only a little, and therefore have little reason to be grateful?

ENTIRELY APPROPRIATE

The same thing happened with another woman, a friend of Jesus' with no checkered past, just a heart of love for the Lord. She too did the grossly improper thing, crossing social and gender barriers to enter an all-male gathering. Though unwelcome, she nevertheless opened a jar and poured a fragrant, high-priced perfume on Jesus' head. More blessed excess.

When some of the men began to mutter about how inappropriate these actions were, how the perfume cost the equivalent of a year's wages, and how all that money could have been better spent on the poor, Jesus spoke forcefully: "Leave her alone. . . . Why are you bothering her? She has done a beautiful thing to me" (Mark 14:6). The Greek word translated "good" is *kalos,* meaning "fine," "beautiful," "elegant." It is used in the Septuagint, the Greek Old Testament, to describe what pleases God, what gives him joy. Jesus thus judged her "excess" as entirely appropriate and said of it something he said of no other human act: "I tell you the truth, wherever the gospel is preached throughout the world, what she has done will also be told, in memory of her" (Mark 14:9). And indeed it has been told, countless times in every corner of the earth. That's how highly God regards joyful gratitude. In language that echoes the words of Communion—"do this in my memory"—he blessed the expression of her gratitude as corresponding perfectly to the grace shown her and therefore worthy of universal remembrance.

The Bible says it is fitting to offer praise as a kind of sacrifice. "Through Jesus, therefore, let us continually offer to God a sacrifice of praise" (Hebrews 13:15). The picture is from the sacrificial system of the temple, which shows us that God's extravagant gestures demand extravagant praise. Whether lambs or goats, the sacrifices had three things in common. First, they were to be the first and the best of a person's flock. Second, a sacrifice had to be given in total abandon, nothing held back. Death is total. Finally, the point of the sacrifice was not death but life— life released through death, for the life of the animal was in the blood (Leviticus 17:11). A sacrifice of praise is living sacrifice (Romans 12:1), our best given up in total abandon to God—like those women, like Jesus. What would our worship services look and sound like if we took this seriously? What would lives lived this way do to the world?

In Charles Spurgeon's little book *Eccentric Preachers,* he tells of the nineteenth-century preacher Billy Bray of Cornwall, England. Billy came to Christ as an alcoholic miner at age twenty-nine and was immediately filled with a grateful joy that makes my Uncle Albert seem restrained. He said, "In an instant the Lord made me so happy I cannot express what I felt. I shouted for joy. Everything looked new to me; the people, the fields, the cattle, the trees. I was like a new man in a new world." He became a Methodist and started to preach with such enthusiasm that people called him a madman. Billy laughed it off and said, "They mean 'glad man'!" Thus a fruitful forty-four-year career of evangelism, church planting and caring for orphans was launched in joy.

Billy's joy affected his walking. He said, "I can't help praising God. As I go along the street I lift one foot up and it seems to say 'Glory!' and I lift the other, and it seems to say, 'Amen!' And they keep on like that all the time I'm walking." Billy fasted each week every Sunday afternoon until Sunday evening. If he was urged to eat something, he would exclaim, "On Sunday I get my breakfast and dinner from the King's table, two good meals too."

Even death was powerless to rob him of his delight in God. When he lost his beloved wife, Joey, he jumped around the room shouting, "Bless the Lord! My dear Joey is gone up with the bright ones! Glory! Glory! Glory!" It was the same when he found out that he too was dying. He shouted, "Glory! Glory to God! I shall soon be in heaven." Then he told the doctor, "When I get up there, shall I give them your compliments doctor, and tell them you will be coming, too?" His last word was, "Glory!"

Spurgeon concludes, "It does not seem so very horrible after all, that a man should be eccentric."[3]

NAZIRITES OF JOY

The Nazirites were people of Israel who separated themselves from others in a vow of consecration to the Lord. For the duration of their vow they did not cut their hair and abstained from alcoholic beverages. Their lifestyle wasn't for everybody, but their devotion was. Their eccentric presence was a reminder of commitment to the Lord that applied to all the people.

I think God sometimes sends Nazirities of joy to his church, not so much that we should copy their behavior as come to desire their joy in God. The way Billy Bray expressed joy belonged to him alone. But the joy he found in God is for everybody. There are not different brands of joy, just as there are not different brands of God.

Another example: On the night of Monday, November 23, 1654, the great scientist and mathematician Blaise Pascal had a mystical encounter with God. With as much precision as his scientific mind could muster, he tried to record what he had experienced. He kept the account sewed in his clothing until his death, probably carrying it wherever he went. He wrote of the transcendent joy of the God of joy.

God of Abraham, God of Isaac, God of Jacob,
not of the philosophers and scholars.
Certainty, certainty, heartfelt, joy, peace.
God of Jesus Christ . . .
Forgetfulness of the world and everything, except God.

He is to be found only in the ways taught in the Gospel.
Greatness of the human soul.
"Righteous father, the world hath not known Thee, but I have
　known Thee."
Joy, joy, joy, tears of joy.[4]

Pascal was a Nazirite, an eccentric of joy. We shouldn't feel cheated if
we've never encountered God the way he did, nor should we try to rep-
licate his experience. Pascal's experience was not that of every believer,
but the God he met and the joy he received are the same. His words
should awaken in us a desire for the God who gives such joy. Each of us
is a unique and different instrument to be tuned by the same Spirit to
sing his praise.

The big difference between the joy Pascal and Bray knew and the joy
I typically know is that joy seized them. They could no more help what
came over them than a surfer can help the waves coming in from the
ocean. And like a surfer, they could only ride it when it came. Happy are
those for whom joy comes in this way. My joy isn't usually that kind. It
comes and goes, waxes and wanes. Sometimes joy sweeps me off my
feet, but more often it courts me and asks for a decision.

DESCRIBED AND PRESCRIBED

Joy is a choice. In fact, Scripture commands it. True, as Bray and Pascal
show us, it is sometimes an irresistible influx of God's favor. He can give
joy just as he gives all his other graces, and we can do no more—or
less—than receive what he gives:

> You have filled my heart with greater joy
> 　　than when their grain and new wine abound. (Psalm 4:7)

> You have made known to me the path of life;
> 　　you will fill me with joy in your presence,
> 　　with eternal pleasures at your right hand. (Psalm 16:11)

> The precepts of the LORD are right,
> 　　giving joy to the heart. (Psalm 19:8)

The apostle Peter spoke of joy as a given in his first epistle, the natural outcome of believing the gospel: "Though you have not seen him, you love him; and even though you do not see him now, you believe in him and are filled with an inexpressible and glorious joy, for you are receiving the goal of your faith, the salvation of your souls" (1 Peter 1:8-9). But joy is also prescribed. Joy is both what one feels and what one does.

Shout with joy to God, all the earth!
   Sing the glory of his name;
      make his praise glorious! (Psalm 66:1-2)

Jesus commands joy in the most uncongenial of situations—when we're being persecuted. How else could joy exist in the midst of oppression except as obedience to a command, not what we feel but what we do? Jesus says the proper response is to "rejoice in that day and leap for joy, because great is your reward in heaven" (Luke 6:23).

The Lord also commands his disciples to redirect their joy. It's quite a trick to cease being joyful for one thing in order to be joyful for another. But Jesus clearly believes they can make that choice. They've been thrilled to exercise power in the service of the kingdom, to see demons obey when they use the name of Jesus. But their joy is misdirected, he says: "Do not rejoice that the spirits submit to you, but rejoice that your names are written in heaven" (Luke 10:20). When he says this, he himself is filled with the joy of the Holy Spirit and thanks his Father that it is his "good pleasure"—his joy—to hide himself from those who think themselves wise and learned and to reveal himself to "little children" (Luke 10:21). Everyone is involved in this command to be joyful—not just the disciples, but the Father, the Son and the Holy Spirit!

Two other classic New Testament texts on the command to be joyful are found in Paul's letters. He issues back-to-back commands in Philippians 4:4: "Rejoice in the Lord always. I will say it again: Rejoice!" And 1 Thessalonians 5:16-18 is just as succinct: "Be joyful always; pray continually; give thanks in all circumstances, for this is God's will for you in Christ Jesus."

JOY IS A SPIRITUAL DISCIPLINE

Since joy is a command, we may also see it as a spiritual discipline, something we choose to do constantly in order to do it better. That's how discipline works. For a competitive swimmer, to swim daily is to swim better. A basketball player practices shooting free throws in order to shoot free throws more skillfully.

The realm of the Spirit is like that. Joy is a fruit of the Holy Spirit; it's what we exhibit when the Spirit has control. The Spirit cannot be controlled—as Jesus said, the Spirit is like the wind. But we can spread our sails to catch the wind when it blows. That's what the spiritual disciplines do for a Christian. By engaging in them we position ourselves to give the Holy Spirit maximum access. The spiritual disciplines do for our souls what a camera shutter does for the film inside. Strictly speaking, cameras don't make pictures. Only light makes pictures as it gains access to the film in the camera. A spiritual discipline positions our soul to receive the light that changes us into the image of Jesus Christ.

The discipline of joy is a discipline of thanksgiving. We are to give thanks and rejoice no matter what—to rejoice in order to be joyful. To one bereft of joy, this may seem like telling the crippled to walk by walking. But the blessed and liberating command to just do it can unlock the coldest of hearts; there is a compassionate genius in the discipline of joy: "Be joyful always; pray continually; give thanks in all circumstances, for this is God's will for you in Christ Jesus" (1 Thessalonians 5:16-18).

Pascal gave similar counsel to skeptics who wanted to know if Christianity was true. The way they could find out, he said, was to behave "just as if they did believe."[5] Philosopher Peter Kreeft explains Pascal's advice as the "feedback principle" in action. Sometimes when damage to the brain has crippled a person's limbs, therapists can begin to heal the brain by exercising the arms or legs. Gradually new neural networks are formed and the brain regains some control. External behavior can change internal realities. The skeptic who has not been convinced by arguments and proofs can know the truth by acting as if he knew it. She can obey in order to believe. The heart has eyes, and they are opened by exposure to the light.[6]

Jesus taught this principle when he said, "Anyone who *wants to do* the will of God will know whether my teaching is from God or is merely my own" (John 7:17 NLT, emphasis added). Do we want to know if Jesus is true? The key is to first know something about ourselves: Are we willing to obey him? If the answer is yes, we will indeed know him; if it is no, we won't. "Obedience is the opener of eyes," wrote George MacDonald. "We don't see in order to obey; we obey in order to see."[7]

SUFFICIENT REASONS FOR JOY

Joy can be commanded because it is based on objective reality, not a subjective feeling. The realities of God, his Son and the gospel go deeper than any experience of pain or pleasure. For what other reason than Jesus can the faithful suffer joyfully? He said that to suffer for righteousness is a blessed thing and we should rejoice when the opportunity arises (Matthew 5:10-12).

From the beginning Christians took this to heart and suffered joyfully. The apostles were flogged for their testimony and left the prison "rejoicing because they had been counted worthy of suffering disgrace for the Name" (Acts 5:41). Flogging was not a generic beating. It was a brutal and painful punishment consisting of thirty-nine lashes with rods or a whip. Someone who had endured a flogging emerged wounded, bloody and depleted for days, even weeks. But inexplicably there was joy in the wounds of these apostles. Paul and Silas are unforgettable in the Philippian dungeon, having been stripped, flogged and put in stocks. And they're singing (Acts 16:22-25). How could this be?

Clearly their joy came from something deeper than circumstances. Our English word *happy* gives itself away. Its root is the Latin *hap,* which means "chance." Typically for us, joy is happiness, what we feel when circumstances are pleasant. But Christian joy is anchored in the facts of faith, to be trusted no matter the circumstances: Christ has come, Christ has died, Christ is risen and coming again. My sins are forgiven, my hope is sure. As the Heidelberg Catechism states, "I belong, body and soul, in life and in death" to my faithful Savior, Jesus Christ. Nothing can separate me from his love. These are the fixed quantities amid changing circumstances. These are the soil of joy.

God commands joy because he has given us reason to be grateful. Only spiritual obtuseness gets in the way. This is what George Herbert was lamenting when he prayed,

> Thou that hast given so much to me,
> Give one thing more, a grateful heart. . . .
> Not thankful when it pleaseth me,
> As if Thy blessings had spare dayes;
> But such a heart whose pulse may be
> Thy praise.[8]

Herbert saw that his spiritual poverty was such that he needed not only God's gifts but also the gift to recognize them and be grateful.

The church I pastored in New Jersey funded the translation of the *Jesus* film into the language of a primitive people who live in the jungles of East Asia. Since a repressive Muslim government rules them, I won't identify them more precisely. These people had never heard of Jesus or seen a motion picture. At the premiere of this movie their joy—and that of the missionaries witnessing it—knew no bounds.

When the people saw this good man who healed sick people and spoke tenderly with children held without trial and beaten, they came unglued. They began to shout and shake their fists at the screen. When nothing happened, they turned to the missionary running the projector. Maybe he was responsible for this injustice! He had to stop the film to explain that the story wasn't over yet. So they reluctantly settled down to watch.

Next was the crucifixion. Again the people came apart. They threw themselves on the ground and wailed. There was so much noise the missionary again stopped the film to explain that there was more to come. Again they composed themselves.

Then came the resurrection. This time the missionary had to stop the movie not because of anger but because of the celebration that erupted. A party broke out with dancing, singing and backslapping. They were given reason enough to be grateful, and therefore to be joyful.

We have been given the same reasons. "Thou that hast given so much to me, Give one thing more, a grateful heart." Such sad words these are, that we who have been given every reason for joy can be so joyless. So God commands it: when we cease to see as clearly as those wise and simple tribespeople, we are to rejoice anyway—that we may see better.

CONVERTED TO JOY

I vividly remember the day I became a Christian, and I clearly remember the moment I began to understand joy. I'm sorry to say the two events are separated by many years. I was converted to Christ when I was about nine years old, and I was converted to joy when I was fifty. One year I didn't want to go back to work after my vacation. I was burdened with the problems of the church and depressed over struggles in my family. But I gritted my teeth, pointed the car toward home and went back, grimly determined to be obedient to God and do my job. This attitude continued for two weeks. Then one night in a prayer meeting the Lord spoke to me. The words were harsh, but the tone was tender. He said, "I don't need this from you, Ben. If you can't serve me joyfully, don't call it service. You dishonor me with your ingratitude. Change your attitude or get another job."

That night the meaning of joy became clear to me: while joy is a gift, it is also a choice. I had been passive about joy. God was telling me he had already given me all I needed to be joyful because joy comes out of being grateful—and if my faith tells me anything, it tells me that I have every reason to be very, very grateful. Only spiritual obtuseness disconnects this reality from my emotions. Every day I have reason to behave just as those primitive people did in the jungle when they saw the Jesus story for the first time. So I pray, with no small embarrassment, "Thou that hast given so much to me, Give one thing more, a grateful heart."

2

JOY BUSTERS

Still they stood there doubting, filled with joy and wonder.

LUKE 24:41 (NLT)

H. L. Mencken defined Puritanism as "the haunting fear that somebody, somewhere may be happy." His accusation of joylessness is unfair when applied to the Puritans themselves, especially the early ones, who were anything but gloomy. But it may be valid for somber Christians who find it hard to connect the joyful implications of their faith with the realities of their life. For these people, seriousness and joy don't mix—people like the wife in John Steinbeck's *East of Eden*, "a tight hard little woman humorless as a chicken. She had a dour Presbyterian mind and a code of morals that pinned down and beat the brains out of nearly everything that was pleasant to do."[1]

Joy is what we experience when we are grateful for the grace given us. Gratitude and joy are natural responses to God's grace, its twin children. Gratitude and joy follow grace like thunder follows lightning. Why, then, do they come so hard for some? One reason is our collection of attitudes and behaviors that pin down and beat the brains out of joy—the things I call "joy busters."

LIKE A WOUNDED HAND

One joy buster is past pain and disappointment. The disciples must have been struggling with this when they saw Christ alive after his crucifixion.

Curiously, Luke writes, "Still they stood there doubting, filled with joy and wonder" (Luke 24:41 NLT). Why so ambivalent, so tentative? The reason isn't complicated: the pain of their loss had been so great it made it nearly unbearable to believe again. Their faith was like a wounded hand—they wanted to grip the truth, but it hurt when they did.

Bruce Springsteen sang a song about Bill Horton, a man with a wounded hand. Horton was a restless man, a wanderer, afraid to risk love. Every choice he made was a kind of cost-benefit analysis in which he weighed his need against what he might lose if he chose wrong. He lived cautiously, carefully. He came to love a woman, but it terrified him. Horton had the word *love* tattooed on his right hand and the word *fear* on his left, and which of them held his fate wasn't exactly clear. Loss can do that to us. Fear of the future based on the pain of the past can kill love and joy. It can make us afraid to get up for fear of the crash coming down.

In the summer of 1969 I had to face the fact that a girl I had loved for five years didn't care for me the way I cared for her. It was no failure on her part, but it was a galling realization for me. I had invested so much hope in our future that when it became clear there would be no future, I was angry and bitter—at her, at myself for believing in us so much, for being vulnerable, but mostly at God. Though I would never have said it out loud, I had believed deep in my soul that if I lived a good life and faithfully obeyed his commandments, he owed me one big favor. Not a lot of favors, but one big one. She was the big one. And when God appeared to renege on the tacit agreement I felt we had, I was mad.

So for the next year and a half I went out and systematically broke the commandments I had formerly kept. I did just about everything my Sunday school teachers had said would destroy me. I gained a reputation for being the guy to be with for a good time. Wild and crazy times, but there was no joy in me. I had fear tattooed on my heart.

It's a long story how God in his mercy pulled up the bitter root in my soul and brought me to repentance. But he did, and two years after the summer of 1969 God brought me the wonderful woman who has been my wife ever since. Another two years passed, and one day I was listening to a silly love song on the radio. It was one of those how-hard-it-would-be-for-him-to-lose-her songs. I didn't even like the song, but the Holy Spirit came to me through it (oh, the humility of God!) and showed me how much I was holding back from my wife. Huge parcels of my soul were fenced off with barbed wire. I didn't want anyone in them, but as I listened to that stupid song I began to weep and let her in. And joy came with her. Then came a greater realization: not only had I kept my wife out, but I had kept God out as well. I hadn't trusted him to be faithful, either. An even greater joy came when I let God in.

What do we do when paralyzed by the bitterness and fear of past pain? The first step is to acknowledge its existence, to admit the reason we may be unable—or unwilling, really—to know joy. Name it. There is power there. Second, we ask God to change our hearts. That may be a bold move, for it's strange how attached we can become to bitterness and fear. Maybe we secretly relish the indignation and self-righteousness that follow a sense of injustice. If we're not quite ready to ask God to change us, we can follow the advice of the nineteenth-century preacher F. B. Meyer. He would often encourage his listeners to ask God to make them willing to be willing!

THE MYOPIA OF THE MOMENT

Another joy buster is the myopia of the moment, where we get so caught up in the depressing present we can't see a hopeful future. But biblical joy is about our whole life, not just a moment. Salvation involves our past, present and future—our entire life, not just a part. An Anglican bishop was accosted on the sidewalk by an overzealous street preacher. "Are you saved?" the preacher demanded. The bishop answered, "More than that, sir. I have been saved, I am being saved, and I will be saved." There are no moments that contain all the others. Only God contains all moments, for he is the God who "was, and is, and is to come" (Revelation 4:8). And because he is in all of these, he can redeem us in each.

The implications for joy are profound. The Bible says the three great lasting qualities are faith, hope and love (1 Corinthians 13:13). Theologian Emil Brunner has observed that these three give meaning to the three tenses of life. Faith speaks to the past, for it trusts that Christ has paid for all our sins—"I have been saved." Hope speaks to our future, for God has promised that we will spend an eternity of joy in his presence (Psalm 16:11)—"I will be saved." Love speaks to our present—"I am being saved." Because the past and the future are guaranteed, we can be free from guilt (the past) and fear (the future) and liberated to love, which we can only do in the present. Joy is the first fruit of love, the deep gladness that in spite of what is now, what will be is sure to be wonderful, "not worth comparing with the glory that will be revealed in us" (Romans 8:18). This is the perspective that sets our vision straight and cures spiritual myopia.

The word *nevertheless* is a great gospel word. God looks at our sin and says, "Nevertheless." It's a great joy word too. Like God, in a way, we can look at our devastating circumstances and know nevertheless that it will turn out okay in the end. Everything else is just details—fleeting, ephemeral details. Things like cancer, depression, divorce and lousy jobs are abominable in the short term. But they are not the final word. They will pass away; our eternal destiny is unshakable.

FUNDAMENTALLY SOUND

When my circumstances aren't agreeable, I practice a little spiritual discipline that keeps me in joy nevertheless. When someone asks me how I am I'll answer, "Other than the fact that my sins are forgiven and that I'm going to live in heaven eternally in the joy of God, I'm not doing too well." The look on the questioner's face always amuses me, and it usually lifts the cloud a bit. Sometimes I'll just answer, "Fundamentally sound." I may be superficially bummed out, sad, frustrated, angry—whatever!— but that's the worst I can say about it. It's surface only.

Two test cases illustrate this principle in action. The first involves grief. In 1871, Horatio Spafford lost his son and all his real estate holdings in the great Chicago fire. Two years later, desiring a rest, he booked passage on a ship to England for himself, his wife and four daughters. Last-minute business commitments forced him to stay back and send his wife and daughters ahead. En route, the ship collided with another ship and sank in twelve minutes. All four daughters drowned. Mrs. Spafford cabled her husband just two words: "Saved alone." When he sailed over to meet her, the captain of the ship pointed out the approximate place where the disaster had taken place. He went into his cabin and wrote the words of what has become the famous hymn "It Is Well with My Soul." Note how the verses touch on the past, present and future of the gospel and affirm the way faith, hope and love deliver us from spiritual myopia.

> When peace, like a river, attendeth my way,
> When sorrows like sea billows roll—
> Whatever my lot, Thou hast taught me to say,
> It is well, it is well with my soul.
>
> Tho Satan should buffet, tho trials should come,
> Let this blest assurance control,
> That Christ hath regarded my helpless estate,
> And hath shed his own blood for my soul.
>
> My sin—O the bliss of this glorious tho't—
> My sin, not in part, but the whole,
> Is nailed to the cross, and I bear it no more:
> Praise the Lord, praise the Lord, O my soul!
>
> And, Lord, haste the day when my faith shall be sight,
> The clouds be rolled back as a scroll;
> The trump shall resound and the Lord shall descend,
> "Even so"—it is well with my soul.[2]

"It is well with my soul" was Spafford's way of saying, "Other than the fact that my sins are forgiven and that I'm going to live in heaven eternally in the joy of God, I'm not doing too well. But I'm fundamentally sound."

A more exacting test of rejoicing in difficult circumstances is depression. William Cowper (1731-1800), the great Christian poet and mystic, suffered most of his life from what today we would call bipolar disorder or manic depression. At age thirty-two he tried to poison himself but failed. He then decided to throw himself into the Thames, so he hired a horse-drawn cab to drive him there. It was one of the foggiest nights of the year, and the cabby drove for more than an hour and couldn't find the bridge. In disgust, Cowper got out of the cab to walk to the bridge. After much wandering, he discovered that he had walked in a circle and ended up back at his own doorstep. The next morning he fell on his knife, but the handle broke. He tried to hang himself but was cut down, unconscious but alive.

Some days later he was reading the Bible and came to faith in Christ. But he struggled with depression until his death. The last hymn he wrote before descending into a depression that lasted the final seven years of his life was "God Moves in a Mysterious Way." His own title was "Light Shining out of Darkness." It expressed faith that everything was fundamentally sound despite the darkness of the moment, and despite the fact that the "moment" lasted seven years. All that God does, Cowper asserted, he does with infinitely wise love.

> God moves in a mysterious way
> His wonders to perform;
> He plants his footsteps in the sea,
> And rides upon the storm.
>
> Deep in unfathomable mines
> Of never-ending skill,
> He treasures up his bright designs,
> And works his sovereign will.
>
> Ye fearful saints, fresh courage take,
> The clouds ye so much dread,
> Are big with mercy, and shall break
> In blessings on your head.
>
> Judge not the Lord by feeble sense,
> But trust him for his grace:
> Behind a frowning providence
> He hides a smiling face.

His purposes will ripen fast
Unfolding every hour;
The bud may have a bitter taste
But sweet will be the flower.

Blind unbelief is sure to err,
And scan his work in vain;
God is his own interpreter
And he will make it plain.[3]

Cowper's dear friend John Newton, with noteworthy prescience, somehow understood that depression can be a physical disorder. He preached at his funeral: "He was one of those who came out of great tribulations. He suffered much here . . . but eternity is long enough to make amends for all. For what is all he endured in this life, when compared with the rest which remaineth for the children of God?"[4]

THE CAPACITY FOR ECSTASY

Another joy buster is the fear of losing control. Jesus said the Holy Spirit is like the wind, mysterious and unmanageable (John 3:8). If we feel the need for control at all times, joy may seem like a threat because it comes from an unmanageable God. The word *ecstasy* is not a synonym for *joy,* but its roots are instructive. Ecstasy comes from *ek,* "out of," and *stasis,* "place." The capacity for ecstasy is the capacity to be moved out of place. The ecstatic dimension of joy is the ability to be moved, shifted, taken from one element into another.

Psalm 126 is a great psalm of joy, and it touches on the ecstatic as the psalmist looks back to a great time in Israel's history.

When the LORD brought back the captives to Zion,
  we were like men who dreamed.
Our mouths were filled with laughter,
  our tongues with songs of joy. (Psalm 126:1-2)

Some may argue that laughter can be a restrained little titter, but I don't think so. Laughter is laughter; titters are titters. *Laughter* is an ecstasy word; *titter* is a control word. I like that their mouths were filled with laughter. Picture a mouth crammed with a big bite from a peanut butter sandwich. It's practically impossible to speak an intelligible word and the only thing to do is chew. The Israelites' mouths were filled this way with laughter, and their tongues were weighed down with songs of joy, or "joyful shouting" in the Hebrew. Laughter and shouting rule! Peanut butter for the soul!

The psalmist wants more, which is the way it is with joy. Even as it deeply satisfies, it makes us ravenous for more.

> Restore our fortunes, O LORD,
>   like streams in the Negev.
> Those who sow in tears
>   will reap with songs of joy.
> He who goes out weeping,
>   carrying seed to sow,
> will return with songs of joy,
>   carrying sheaves with him. (Psalm 126:4-6)

This psalm mentions two ways joy can come. One is for it to sprout slowly and richly, as a seed does in a field: sowing tears and reaping joy, seeds turning gradually into bushels and bundles. But another way for joy to come is suddenly and tumultuously, like streams in the Negev. The Negev is a desert and streams are rare. When they do come they bring flash floods with them. I've stood in a desert, sweltering in blistering dry heat, and watched thunderheads pour rain on a mountain miles away. I know better than to stand in a dry streambed when that happens, for when the water comes it will roar down, a watery wall that carries away everything in its path. Joy can be that way too.

Which kind of joy do you want? True, joy is joy either way, and both bring an abundance of delight. But if we put stipulations on the way God comes to us, he may not come at all. Remember, the Holy Spirit is sovereignly unmanageable. He reserves the right to be God and appear when and how he wills.

I was raised to prefer what I call an Aristotelian joy, the golden mean between two extremes. I didn't want what I saw at the local Pentecostal church—too raw and boisterous. Nor did I want the kind of thing I saw in my more liturgically oriented friends—too buttoned-down and cerebral. If the liturgicals were an aged Cabernet, the Pentecostals were tequila. I was a Calvinistic Baptist: I wanted grape juice. I wanted good doctrinal preaching, minimal body involvement, a rousing hymn and damp (not wet) eyes once in a while. I wanted joy in regular doses that I could count on and, above all, I wanted control. If inoculation is getting just enough of the real thing not to get the real thing, then I was inoculated against joy.

When the bottom fell out of my life in the summer of 1969, I traded grape juice for strong drink—literally. One morning I woke up with a hangover, shuffled into my kitchen and made coffee. As I sat on the sofa and sipped, I stared blankly at a pile of magazines on the table. Underneath was a Bible I hadn't cracked in months. The sight made me think about praying. But what about? I instinctively didn't want to go near anything like the hallowing of God's name, or confession. So I chose something I naively deemed safe: I began to give God thanks. Big mistake.

My gratitude was general at first; I brought up things like good weather and music. But soon, with a welling up in my breast I remember still, my thanks grew more intense and specific. I thanked God for the coffee and the cup, the magazines and the knives and forks in the sink, the napkins. As I poured out my thanks, an unbidden, inexplicable and undeserved joy began to trickle and then roar into my fuzzy mind. Life was so good! God was so good to give life! Tears came and more words, and then I felt myself move beyond normal language into something else, something like . . . like . . . With a jerk, I noticed that whatever was coming out of my mouth sounded like what I had heard at the Pentecostal church. I caught myself and stopped immediately—just in time, I thought.

For years I regretted aborting that birth. I came to believe, and still do, that God was trying to give me real drink, not the cheap joy substitutes I was imbibing. How gracious and kind of him. How foolishly fearful of me. How joyless. How incapable of being moved.

Roderick Caesar is the pastor of Bethel Gospel Tabernacle, a black Pentecostal church in Jamaica Queens, New York. He is a remarkable man of God and someone I am proud to call a friend. In 1992 he invited me to preach to his people. During the song service that Sunday I noticed that the people were definitely not Aristotelian in their joy. As I stood up front with Roderick, I did my white best to move with them. They all smiled at me in a big way and I felt very cool, very free, very soulful. Roderick leaned toward my ear and said, "You know why they're smiling, don't you?" Though I thought I did, I said no, I didn't. He chuckled and said, "It's because you don't know how to move." I laughed, but my face turned red. Then I looked at their smiles again. It was okay with them that I couldn't move. They were smiling at me, not laughing, and I have eternity to learn how to let go and move with them in the joy of God.

The Bible says, "Do not get drunk on wine, which leads to debauchery. Instead, be filled with the Spirit" (Ephesians 5:18). The coupling of these ideas—being drunk with wine and filled with the Spirit—isn't random. Both conditions are forms of being moved, of coming decisively under the influence of something else, of ecstasy, of *ekstasis*. Drunkenness imitates and kills joy. Those who must be in control will know neither influence.

SPIRITUAL AMNESIA

The biggest joy buster of all is a bad memory. To forget what to be thankful for is to forget why to be joyful. So there is an urgency in the Scriptures to remember. David even talks to himself about it.

> Praise the LORD, O my soul;
>   all my inmost being, praise his holy name.
> Praise the LORD, O my soul,
>   and forget not all his benefits. (Psalm 103:1-2)

The New Living Translation captures the force of David's self-talk when it translates verse 2, "Praise the Lord, I tell myself, and never forget the good things he does for me." What is it he is urging himself never to forget? Plenty.

> Who forgives all your sins
>   and heals all your diseases,
> who redeems your life from the pit
>   and crowns you with love and compassion,
> who satisfies your desires with good things
>   so that your youth is renewed like the eagle's. (Psalm 103:3-5)

Only the very dull or the nearly dead would not be moved to deep thankfulness and joy at the memory of these things.

The cultivation of memory was important to Jesus too. He told us to eat a meal, to break the bread and drink the wine, "in remembrance of me" (Luke 22:19; 1 Corinthians 11:23-26). At the heart of Christian worship is a meal for the stimulation of memory. We remember two things: our great sinfulness and misery, and the price Christ's love paid on the cross to save us. Our misery is measured by the cross; our gratitude and joy should be too.

When we lose the memory of our sin and God's mercy, we forget why to be joyful. His grace ceases to be a heart-stopping miracle and degenerates into a merely pleasant feature on the religious landscape.

It's like what happened in R. C. Sproul's Old Testament class his first year of teaching. There were 250 first-year students in Sproul's class. He informed them that the assignments included three papers, the first due September 30, the second October 30 and the third November 30. He emphasized that each of the papers must be turned in no later than noon on the due date. An F grade would be assigned to any late papers, no exceptions. "Does everybody understand?" he asked. "Oh, yes," they all said.

On September 30, 25 of the 250 students didn't have their papers ready. They begged for mercy from Dr. Sproul, for an extension, please, please, please. They were, he said, "in a posture of abject humility," pleading for grace. And he gave grace, but with the warning, "Don't let it happen again. Remember the next assignment is due October 30, and I want those papers in." They promised yes, absolutely.

October 30 came and this time fifty students were without papers. They stood outside his office in terror. Really, they didn't budget their time well; it was midterms and homecoming and they were swamped—one more chance, please. Sproul yielded to their entreaties, but with another warning: "Don't let it happen again."

It did. On November 30, a hundred students came casually into class minus their papers. They weren't worried in the least. They told professor Sproul to chill out, they'd get their papers to him in a couple of days.

Sproul took out his black grading book and his pen and asked a student, "Johnson, where's your term paper?" Johnson said he didn't have it, so Sproul wrote an F in the book. He asked another student the same question: "Greenwood, where's your paper?" He didn't have it, either. Sproul wrote another F in the book.

The class was furious! As one person, they shouted, "That's not fair."

Sproul bristled. He said, "Johnson, did I just hear you say that's not fair?"

Johnson replied, "Yes, that's not fair."

Sproul answered, "Well, I don't ever want to be thought of as unfair or unjust. Johnson, it's justice that you want?" Johnson said yes.

"Okay," said Sproul, "If I recall, you were late last time, weren't you?" Johnson said yes.

"Then I'll go back and change that grade to an F." He erased his passing grade and gave him an F. Then he looked at the class and asked, "Is there anybody else who wants justice?" There were no takers.[5]

We do the same thing with God when we forget what it cost him to save us. Like Sproul's students, we forget the astonishing mercy of forgiveness and come to think of our salvation as our right, God's obligation to us. But every breath we take is because of his mercy. We love because he first loved us. We hope because he promises. Paul asked the Corinthians, "What do you have that you did not receive? And if you did receive it, why do you boast as though you did not?" (1 Corinthians 4:7). Indeed. One form of boasting is a life of quiet ingratitude, and it's not only wrong, it's a joyless way to live.

For God's sake and our own, we must not forget to remember what Os Guinness calls "the once and might have been"—our wretchedness before God's grace, our blessedness in God's grace. Only when we remember to say thank you for such amazing grace can there be joy.

Thomas à Kempis was a happy man, joyful in the service of Christ, because he understood this. He prayed,

> My God and my love, you are mine and I am yours. Deepen your love in me, O Lord, that I may learn how joyful it is to serve you. Let your love take hold of me and raise me above myself, that I may be filled with devotion because of your goodness. Then I will sing a song to you of love. I will follow you, and my soul will never grow tired of praising you. Let me love you more than myself, and love myself only for your sake. Let me love all others in you and for you, as your law of love commands.[6]

> Amen.

THE HAPPY GOD

*I have no understanding of a long-faced Christian.
If God is anything, he must be joy.*

JOE E. BROWN

*O*ne day when my children were small, I was dusting the living room furniture. Music was playing, Beethoven's Fifth as I recall, and I began to move to the music as I worked. The more I worked and listened, the more vigorously and flamboyantly I danced. Thinking no one could see, I leapt and twirled through the room without embarrassment. I've been told I look like a bear on roller skates when I dance, but I was having fun.

Gradually I became aware of eyes looking at me—very little eyes. I detected my four-year-old hiding behind the sofa and beaming with delight. After looking around to make sure no one else was watching, I invited him to join in the dance. Around the room we danced, leaping over chairs, running across the coffee table, jumping on the sofa—something he normally would be spanked for doing. We shouted and giggled and sang arias in made-up languages. I finally had to sit down, exhausted. But he continued, and I applauded his mighty maneuvers.

I wish you could have seen the look of unabashed pleasure and joy on my son's face as he danced and soaked up his daddy's praise. He was acting as a true child of his father, receiving and giving pleasure as he danced with and for me. He honored me with his joyful imitation.

Any exploration of joy is incomplete if we do not understand that at its deepest, joy is delight for God and with God—not unlike my dance with my son. Failure to understand this is another joy buster, this one theological: a shrunken and unbiblical view of God. God himself is greater than any of the graces he gives. He is grace; he is love. To delight in God is to see something of his excellence and beauty—the splendor of his "Godness"—and to gratefully exult in the sight. God is, after all, the greatest thing going on in the universe; it only follows that to behold him in even the tiniest way is to be delighted.

How incongruous that God's most ardent supporters have sometimes missed this. In her autobiography, Ellen Glasgow spoke of her religious father as a man of rigid rectitude: "He was entirely unselfish, and in his long life he never committed a pleasure."[1] Apparently Martin Luther's good friend Philip Melancthon was the same way. He was so scrupulously attentive to every moral jot and tittle, that one day Luther was exasperated and exclaimed, "Philip, would you just go out and sin a little bit? God deserves to be able to forgive you for something."[2]

Jonathan Edwards was perhaps the greatest theologian and philosopher America has ever produced. With all of his intellectual rigor and exactitude, though, he was also a great enjoyer of God. He wrote of his conversion:

> The first instance I remember of that sort of inward, sweet delight in God and in divine things, that I have lived much in since, was on reading these words, 1 Timothy 1:17: "Now unto the King eternal, immortal, invisible, the only wise God, be honor and glory for ever and ever. Amen." As I read the words, there came into my soul, and was as it were, diffused through it, a sense of the glory of the Divine Being; a new sense, quite different from anything I ever experienced before. Never any words of Scripture seemed to me as these did. I thought with myself, how excellent a Being that was, and how happy I should be, if I might enjoy that God, and be rapt up to Him in Heaven, and be, as it were, swallowed up in Him forever.[3]

A Delightful and Delighted God

Edwards knew he would be happy if swallowed up in God because he believed God to be happy—very happy. Two other passages in 1 Timothy also speak of God's happiness. 1 Timothy 1:11 calls him "the blessed God." 1 Timothy 6:15-16 describes him as "God, the blessed and only Ruler, the King of kings and Lord of lords, who alone is immortal." The Greek word used for "blessed" in this passage was used in other ancient writings to describe the bliss of the gods—those rich, powerful and self-sufficient beings who had whatever they wanted. At its deepest, joy is delight in a delightful and delighted God.

What are the delights of this joyful God? First, God is delighted with what he creates. His joyful enthusiasm fairly bursts through the lines of Psalm 104, the great song of creation. He dresses up for the occasion, wrapping himself "in light as with a garment" before he "stretches out the heavens like a tent" (Psalm 104:2). His mood is playful as he "makes the clouds his chariot / and rides on the wings of the wind" (Psalm 104:3). The creation of the world is a sovereignly earnest, brilliantly rollicking project for the Almighty as he makes waters flow, seasons change, crops spring up, wine gladden, bread satisfy, lions roar and the sea teem with creatures. What fun it all must be for the Lord! So the psalmist exults, "May the glory of the LORD endure forever; / may the LORD rejoice in his works" (Psalm 104:31). Indeed he does rejoice, / for that is who God is; he is the God of joy.

The Bible says that when God finished the work of creation, he was so happy with it that he pronounced it "very good" (Genesis 1:31). Then he rested, which isn't to say he took a nap because he was exhausted. The sense of rest in the Hebrew is that he sat back and savored his work. God thinks so highly of this joyful act of rest and enjoyment that he commanded us to do it too (Genesis 2:1-3; Exodus 20:8-11).

The Extravagant Gesture

As God rested, he surely savored the extravagant immensity of space, as we humans are only beginning to do. In August of 1989, the unmanned spacecraft Voyager 2 sailed 2.8 billion miles to the edge of our solar system and hurtled over the polar icecap of Neptune. In a scientific feat that was called the cosmic equivalent of sinking a 2,260-mile putt, it transmitted to scientists in California astonishing photographs of a strange and stormy world. Voyager 2's images showed a planet covered by a thick haze of helium and hydrogen with 1,500-mile-per-hour winds pushing frozen clouds of methane across its surface. In its southern hemisphere scientists saw a tremendous storm system, a continuous countercyclone as big as the earth in diameter.

Traveling 60,000-plus miles per hour, it took Voyager 2 twelve years just to get to the outer rim of our solar system. Long after it has stopped sending signals to earth, it will still be traveling through space. In the year 40,176 it will likely pass within 1.7 light-years of the star Ross 248, and in the year 296,036 will perhaps come within 4.3 light-years of the star Sirius. Annie Dillard is right: "If the landscape reveals one certainty, it is that the extravagant gesture is the very stuff of creation."[4] Only an exuberant God acts with such lavishness.

Although God delights in extravagance, it can overwhelm us mortals. Pascal described the universe as so immense that its center is nowhere, its circumference everywhere. "The eternal silence of these infinite spaces fills me with dread," he wrote.[5] Why did God create all that space, those incomprehensible distances? What's Neptune for? Or Ross 248? The only answer we have is that it was his sovereign, gracious and imaginative pleasure to create them. The same is true of his forming nine thousand species of birds and millions of varieties of insects. The Bible commands that we rejoice in this joyful God, and as we do, to "tremble before him, all the earth" (Psalm 96:9).

God also delights in himself. The Bible says he has no needs, no holes in his soul to be filled by another being. "I have no need of a bull from your stall / or of goats from your pens, / for every animal of the forest is mine, / and the cattle on a thousand hills" (Psalm 50:9-10). The ancient Hebrews answered their neighbors' mockery with, "Our God is in heaven; / he does whatever pleases him" (Psalm 115:3). Paul set Athenian idolaters straight: "The God who made the world . . . is not served by human hands, as if he needed anything, because he himself gives all men life and breath and everything else" (Acts 17:24-25). A God who needs nothing finds joy within himself, not from any other source.

HOLY AND HAPPY TRINITY

This joy goes deeper than self-sufficiency. Here we tread on mystery, but what a joyful mystery it is. What could more deeply satisfy an infinite Being than another infinite Being? Or rather, two infinite Beings: the Son and Holy Spirit, who with the Father make the Trinity, the Three in One. No human can adequately explain such a Being, but C. S. Lewis's attempt is as good as any:

> Perhaps the most important difference between Christianity and all other religions [is] that in Christianity God is not a static thing—not even a person—but a dynamic, pulsating activity, a life, almost a kind of drama. Almost, if you don't think me irreverent, a kind of dance. The union between the Father and the Son is such a live, concrete thing that this union itself is also a Person. I know that's almost inconceivable, but look at it this way. You know that among human beings, when they get together in a family, or a club, or a trades union, people talk about the "spirit" of that family, or club, or trades union. They talk about its "spirit" because the individual members, when they're together, do really develop particular ways of talking and behaving which they wouldn't have if they were apart. It is as if a sort of communal personality came into existence. Of course it isn't a real person: it is only like a person. But that's just one of the differences between God and us. What grows out of the joint life of the Father and the Son is a real Person, is in fact the Third of three Persons who are God.[6]

The drama, the dance of life within the Godhead is the joyful communion of Father, Son and Holy Spirit. The God who is love is, in himself, a community of love—and joy.

Let me give one illustration of this out of many in the life of Christ. At a critical moment before his crucifixion, Jesus prayed, "Father, the time has come. Glorify your Son, that your Son may glorify you" (John 17:1).

To glorify is not exactly the same as to rejoice, but the actions are related. Only someone who delights in another wants to give glory to the other.

A picture of my wife and children is sitting beside my computer as I type this manuscript. Their faces and the memories they bring so fill me with joy and pride that I want their images beside me as I work. When I pray at my desk each morning, their faces are in my peripheral vision. If you were to come into my study, I would hold the picture up and tell you about each one. My joy in them is not the same as the pride I take in them, but the two are inseparable. So what is the first thing Jesus prays as he approaches the cross? That the Father he loves be celebrated, and that the Father celebrate the Son he loves. Even in death God is delighted to be God.

God is happy with what he creates, joyful in himself and, third, is delighted to make his creatures the same way—in him. The Bible encourages us to think of God as a bridegroom. He told Israel, "As a bridegroom rejoices over his bride, / so will your God rejoice over you" (Isaiah 62:5). This image of God both delights and amazes me. In my vocation as a pastor, I have stood many times with a bridegroom as he waits for his bride to appear at the back of the sanctuary. Since all eyes are on the bride as she walks down the aisle, most people in the congregation aren't aware of the look on the groom's face. I like to peek at him while everyone else is focused on the bride. I usually see in his face a lovely mixture of longing, passion and tenderness tinged with terror. This Adam is in love, thrilled to be joined to his Eve. Is that a little bit how God feels about us, really? He says so in the Bible.

Jesus summed up the purpose of his mission on earth by saying, "I have told you this so that my joy may be in you and that your joy may be complete" (John 15:11). He spent much of his ministry offering word pictures of what that joy looks like. In his famous parable of the prodigal son, we're accustomed to focusing on God as a loving father, which he is. But this story also presents God as the perfect host. When the foolish boy comes home after a season of waste and debauchery, what does he find his dad to be? The judge, the lecturer in ethics? No, he is the host of a magnificent party—proposing toasts, filling glasses, hovering in the kitchen to be sure the roast is perfectly done, the salad crisp and colorful. And when the elder brother refuses to participate, he goes outside to beg him to come in. He says, "But we had to celebrate and be glad" (Luke 15:32). Jesus says God is like that! He says we *have* to celebrate. It's a necessity, not an option.

HE WILL HAVE A PARTY

Perhaps the greatest demonstration of God's desire for us to know joy is that he coaxes those who need him most but seek him least to come and be satisfied. In one of his parables of the kingdom of God, Jesus likens God to a king who sends out invitations to a great feast. Excuse after excuse comes back. No one will come—an unthinkable snub of one so majestic. So what does the king do? He tells his servants to go out in the alleys of the city and the country lanes and "urge anyone you find to come, so that the house will be full" (Luke 14:23 NLT). He will have a party!

C. S. Lewis was thinking of this parable when he wrote of his conversion. Looking back on the struggle that led to this event, he described himself as "the most dejected and reluctant convert in all England."

> I did not then see what is now the most shining and obvious thing; the Divine humility which will accept a convert even on such terms. The Prodigal Son at least walked home on his own feet. But who can duly adore the love which will open the high gates to a prodigal who is brought in kicking, struggling, resentful, and darting his eyes in every direction for a chance of escape?[7]

Those lines are from Lewis's autobiography, which he titled, significantly, *Surprised by Joy.*

The Bible also says God is appalled when people look for joy in the wrong places. He complains about his people's penchant for virtual joys:

> Has a nation ever changed its gods?
>   (Yet they are not gods at all.)
> But my people have exchanged their Glory
>   for worthless idols.

Be appalled at this, O heavens,
　　and shudder with great horror. . . .
My people have committed two sins:
They have forsaken me,
　　the spring of living water,
and have dug their own cisterns,
　　broken cisterns that cannot hold water. (Jeremiah 2:11-12)

In other words, they have preferred things like drink, sex and ambition to infinite joy. God laments his people's obtuseness: "If you would but listen to me, O Israel! / . . . Open wide your mouth and I will fill it. / . . . If my people would but listen to me / . . . you would be fed with the finest of wheat; / with honey from the rock I would satisfy you" (Psalm 81:8-16). Though infinite in his understanding, God just doesn't get how anyone could refuse such joyous generosity.

KINDLING FOR JOY

We must not miss the critical truth that the only place we can discover the God of joy is the Bible, the book John Piper calls "kindling for Christian hedonism."[8] *Hedonism* is his provocative term for a Christian life that delights in God. Piper believes that God is most glorified in us when we are most satisfied in him. If it is true, as the Westminster Shorter Catechism teaches, that the chief end of humankind is to glorify God and enjoy him forever, then the chief way to glorify God is to enjoy him. The Bible is to this joy what kindling is to a fire, for the Bible alone shows us who God is, his character and mighty deeds. How can we delight in God without knowledge of him? How can joyful gratitude follow grace if we don't know what grace is? Ignorance of the God revealed in Scripture is an enemy of joy in the believer—a real joy buster.

To meditate on the God of the Bible is to kindle joy. George Müller believed this. He thought the best thing he could do each day was to get his soul "happy in the Lord" by reading the Word. Cultivating this habit was more important than any service he might render God, he believed, because it was foundational to a life of service.

I saw more clearly than ever, that the first great and primary business to which I ought to attend every day was, to have my soul
happy in the Lord. The first thing to be concerned about was not,
how much I might serve the Lord, how I might glorify the Lord;
but how I might get my soul into a happy state, and how my inner
man may be nourished. . . . I saw that the most important thing I
had to do was to give myself to the reading of the Word of God and
to meditation on it. . . . By the blessing of God I ascribe to this
mode the help and strength which I have had from God to pass in
peace through deeper trials in various ways than I had ever had before. . . . How different when the soul is refreshed and made happy
early in the morning, from what it is when, without spiritual prep-
aration, the service, the trials and the temptations of the day come
upon one![9]

How can we emulate Müller in our quest for joy? First, we can open the
Bible as if we believe everything in it to be true. We can meditate on Scripture expectantly, confident we will find the very thoughts of the God at
whose right hand are eternal pleasures (Psalm 16:11). We can drink daily
draughts from the Book that springs from his river of delights (Psalm 36:8).

THE GOD OF JOY AND THE JOYS OF GOD

Joy is found in a person, not a thing. At its deepest and truest, joy comes
from God himself, not from the things he does for us or the feelings we
get when we sense him near. God's good gifts and the lovely sensations
we experience in him are like footprints in the snow: to fixate on them
is to miss where they lead. If the joys do not lead us to Joy, they are worse
than useless; they are bitterly disappointing since they will pass away. To
make a joy into Joy kills the joy.

My life changed when I began to understand this. I had been operat-
ing under the premise that whatever the joy or pleasure was, then twice
as much would make me feel twice as good—or four times as much, or
ten times as much. I can remember the exact day when I began to see
things differently. I had been in San Diego for business and was planning

to take the train home to Irvine at the end of the day. Two friends picked me up where I had been working downtown and drove me to the train station in Del Mar. Del Mar is a pretty little seacoast town on any day, but on that day it sparkled. The temperature was a perfect seventy-six degrees, the breeze soft and fragrant off the ocean. Children played in the park, surfers rode the emerald waves, seagulls glided.

We had an hour until the train arrived, so we went to a deli and bought lunch: big turkey sandwiches on sourdough bread, chips and salsa, and a bottle of wine. The food tasted exquisite, and our conversation was deep and filled with laughter. The wine gently enhanced all these good sensations—the sights, the sounds, the joys of friendship. I began to feel slightly irritated that the train was nearing and the perfect time would have to end. I started to calculate how I could postpone my return by calling my wife and telling her I would be a little late, a vague lie implying that I was tied up with business. I wanted more conversation, more wine, more food, more sunshine and ocean—more joy. If this much made me feel so good, how much better would more be? How much joy could I extract from the moment by catching a later train home? God have mercy on me for the times I strangled an experience for every last ounce of joy, only to find it dead when I was done.

At that time in my life, however, I was coming to understand that the joys of a day were signposts to Joy, to the good and gracious God who gives people "wine that gladdens the heart . . . / and bread that sustains his heart" (Psalm 104:15)—or deli sandwiches and chips and salsa in a Del Mar park. The reason I loved that day was because it was a little like the God who gave it. To try to seize these things and keep them for myself would be to miss him. Then two terrible things would have happened: First, the little joys that couldn't last anyway would turn bad, and my memory of that day would be tainted with deceit, irresponsibility and gluttony. Second, I would miss the big Joy that can never go bad.

I got on the train, waved to my buddies and went home. The memory remains fresh and sweet, even after twenty years. And I have since gotten to know the God of joy better than I would have had I worshiped the joys of God.

Joy is a person, not a thing. In Paul's letter to the Philippians he repeatedly urges them to "rejoice in the Lord" (4:4). When he speaks of his own great joy, it has nothing to do with the things he once exulted in: his pedigree as the quintessential Jew and Pharisee, his religious purity and zeal. In fact, these former joys have turned to garbage "compared to the surpassing greatness of knowing Christ Jesus" (Philippians 3:8). Such is his delight in Christ that his transcendent ambition is to know him in his fullness, even his sufferings. "I want to know Christ and the power of his resurrection and the fellowship of sharing in his sufferings, becoming like him in his death, and so, somehow, to attain to the resurrection from the dead" (Philippians 3:10-11). Extraordinary! What kind of joy is this? What kind of person can have this effect on people—that if being near him means suffering and death, then let the suffering and death come. It must be a remarkable joy, a remarkable person.

LOVE BETTER THAN LIFE

Paul's experience wasn't unique. Centuries before, the young David, hiding in the hot Judean desert from a murderous Saul, beheld the same joy. But it wasn't his pleasure that pointed to God; it was his pain. He saw in his physical thirst a deeper longing.

> O God, you are my God,
>   earnestly I seek you;
> my soul thirsts for you,
>   my body longs for you,
> in a dry and weary land
>   where there is no water. (Psalm 63:1)

David knew that greater than water, food and life was the God who gave him life and made him for himself. And this gave him cause for great joy and celebration.

> I have seen you in the sanctuary
>   and beheld your power and your glory.
> Because your love is better than life,

my lips will glorify you.
I will praise you as long as I live,
and in your name I will lift up my hands.
My soul will be satisfied as with the richest of foods;
with singing lips my mouth will praise you. (Psalm 63:2-5)

God knows this about himself and invites us to come and eat and drink of him. He is a feast to all who seek him.

Come, all you who are thirsty,
come to the waters;
and you who have no money,
come, buy and eat! . . .
Why spend money on what is not bread,
and your labor on what does not satisfy?
Listen, listen to me, and eat what is good,
and your soul will delight in the richest of fare.
Give ear and come to me;
hear me, that your soul may live. (Isaiah 55:1-3)

Only Jesus, among the founders of the world's religions, says, "I am the bread of life. No one who comes to me will ever be hungry again. Those who believe in me will never thirst. . . . If you are thirsty, come to me! If you believe in me, come and drink! For the Scriptures declare that rivers of living water will flow out from within" (John 6:35; 7:37-38 NLT). The chief way he told us to remember him was by consuming bread and wine that he called his flesh and blood. From the earliest days, the church has eaten this meal with "great joy" (Acts 2:46 NLT).

Saints and mystics throughout history have known this about God too. Bernard of Clairvaux prayed like David: "From the best bliss that earth imparts, we turn unfilled to you again."[10] A man as sober as Jonathan Edwards could speak of being "besotted"—drunk—with God. And even the less saintly and mystical have left picnics in Del Mar and gone home, because his love is better than life.

A Christmas Carol

*What must you know to live and die
in the joy of this comfort?*

The Heidelberg Catechism

$\mathcal{I}$f we were playing a word-association game and I said "catechism," chances are you wouldn't yell "joy!" in response. "Drudgery" and "dry" are more likely, especially if your early religious training involved memorizing one. Someone once told me he thought *catechism* referred to a primitive mechanical device used in a dental office. But a catechism is a teaching document in a question and answer format, and a catechism is what first got me thinking about joy in a way that changed my life. It is also a direct way to address the last of the joy busters: an incomplete gospel. In other words, we may be missing the inexpressible and glorious joy of the gospel because we don't fully understand what its message is.

The catechism I have in mind is a sixteenth-century confession of faith known as the Heidelberg Catechism. I have a calligraphic rendering of the first question and answer framed and hanging in my office. But it is the second question of the Catechism that has changed my life—and made me want to write this book. The two questions go together; you need to hear the first to fully appreciate the second.

Question One: What is your only comfort in life and in death?

Answer: That I am not my own, but belong—body and soul, in life

and death—to my faithful Savior Jesus Christ. He has fully paid for
all my sins with his precious blood, and has set me free from the
tyranny of the devil. He also watches over me in such a way that
not a hair can fall from my head without the will of my Father in
heaven: in fact, all things must work together for my salvation. Because I belong to him, Christ, by his Holy Spirit, assures me of
eternal life and makes me wholeheartedly willing and ready from
now on to work for him.[1]

GUILT, GRACE AND GRATITUDE

Magnificent! All that really matters in life and in death is covered by
those words—identity, security, forgiveness, deliverance and hope. But
how can we know the joy of this comfort? The answer to the second
question is crucial.

Question Two: What must you know to live and die in the joy of
this comfort?

Answer: Three things: first, how great my sin and misery are; second, how I am set free from all my sins and misery; third, how I
am to thank God for such a deliverance.[2]

There it is—the Christian story stated as misery, rescue and joyous
thanksgiving; guilt, grace and gratitude. These three are also joined organically. If the premise of gratitude and joy is the good news, then the
premise of the good news is the bad news. Before joy comes tears. In fact,
joy is frivolous and false without tears. So for the sake of joy we must
think for a while about what the Catechism calls our "sin and misery."

Note first that the word is *sin,* not *sins.* That's because, according to
the Bible, sin is a condition, the state of our souls. Individual sins—
things like murder, adultery, gossip, hate, racism and theft—are the
symptoms of that state. Just as fever, headache and exhaustion are symptoms of the influenza virus, so adultery and gossip are symptoms of the
sin virus. Or to picture it differently, the Greek word for sin, *hamartia,* is
taken from the world of archery and means "to miss the mark." With this

image in mind, Paul declares that "all have sinned and fall short of the glory of God" (Romans 3:23) and the wages, or consequence, of sin is death (Romans 6:23). All our falling short comes from our having fallen short. We aren't sinners because we sin; we sin because we are sinners (Genesis 3:7; John 8:34; Romans 5:12; 6:2, 11, 14; 7:25).

Joy is what we experience when we are grateful for the grace given us. Crucial to joy, then, is understanding sin's relationship to gratitude. Paul describes sin's essence this way: "For although they knew God, they neither glorified him as God *nor gave thanks to him,* but their thinking became futile and their foolish hearts were darkened" (Romans 1:21, emphasis added). The ultimate missing of the mark is refusing to be grateful and give God his due. At its root, sin is ingratitude. Therefore sin by its nature eliminates the very possibility of joy.

The Hard Part Is Getting Them Lost

The word *misery* in the Catechism needs to be understood in this context. Ingratitude darkens the heart and mind, so the misery of sin may not be experienced as pain at all. Being anaesthetized to their true state, sinners may even feel something they call happiness. They are nevertheless miserable, whether they feel it or not, because they are lost and enslaved, darkened in their hearts and futile in their thinking. They cannot know the expansive joy of the infinitely happy God (1 Timothy 1:11). The misery the Catechism speaks of is much more than a subjective state. It is an objective condition.

An evangelist was asked if it was hard to get people saved. He answered, "No, it's not hard to get them saved. The hard part is getting them lost." Part of the misery of being lost is not knowing you are lost. This lack of an awareness of guilt and misery may be a uniquely modern difficulty. C. S. Lewis thought so. He said the "greatest barrier I have met [in explaining the Christian message] is the almost total absence from the minds of my audience of any sense of sin. . . . The early Christian preachers could assume in their hearers . . . a sense of guilt. Thus the Christian message was in those days unmistakably the . . . Good News. It promised healing to those who knew they were sick. We have to convince our hearers of the unwelcome diagnosis before we can expect them to welcome the remedy."[3]

Henry David Thoreau was thinking as a quintessential modern when he was asked if he intended to make his peace with God before he died. He answered, "I didn't know we had ever quarreled."[4] He was thinking as a man in deep, delusional misery. Pascal saw the same kind of self-deception in the seventeenth century when he observed, "We run heedlessly into the abyss after putting something in front of us to stop us seeing it. . . . Being unable to cure death, wretchedness and ignorance, men have decided, in order to be happy, not to think about such things."[5]

It seems illogical, but I think the absence of a deep sense of sin and misery in our modern consciousness is one of the biggest barriers to joy. Without sin and misery the gospel ceases to be a happy thing. It is a good thing, certainly, even a very important thing, but hardly a matter of "inexpressible and glorious joy" (1 Peter 1:8). Jesus the Savior is reduced to Jesus the Supplement, a fitting addition to an already pretty good life. We begin to think we need not so much salvation as advice, encouragement and an improved self-esteem.

LEPROSY OF THE SOUL

The misery of sin is like leprosy. Dr. Paul Brand's research among leprosy victims showed that the disfigurement of lepers was not a direct result of the disease but an indirect effect. Leprosy takes away the sense of pain, so lepers unwittingly do damaging things like putting their hand in fire. They don't know what they're doing—and don't care for the wound—because they don't feel it.[6] Their misery may not be conscious, but it is misery nevertheless and will show itself in burns, infection and deformity. The misery of sin does to the soul what leprosy does to the body.

The scope of our misery is eternal. It isn't merely living a less-than-wonderful life, like driving a Ford Escort instead of a Mercedes Benz. It's a matter of life and death—forever. When God told Adam and Eve they would die if they disobeyed him, he meant it. They didn't drop dead when they disobeyed, but the light went out inside and they eventually did drop into their graves. Death was optional before they fell short and inevitable when they did—a miserable state of affairs.

Sin is everybody's problem, for its depth is measured not by how we compare to one another, but how we stack up next to the glory of God. Picture me and two others poised on the south rim of the Grand Canyon, ready to compete in a long jump contest to the north rim. It's about a mile to the bottom of the canyon and a mile across. The other two competitors are my eighty-seven-year-old mother and a world-class long jumper. My dear mother goes first. She edges up to the rim with her walker, makes her jump and falls to the bottom, two inches from the canyon wall. I go next. I take a run, I leap, and I go fifteen feet beyond my mother's mark. But I end up just a little farther across the bottom of the canyon. The world-class long jumper beats us both by another fifteen feet, but he falls to the bottom too. All three of us end up dead. All three of us fail to land in the place we must be to live. The differences among us are rendered irrelevant by the distance we must cover.

Line up people as disparate morally as Mother Teresa and Adolph Hitler on the rim that separates sinners from the glory of God, and it's the same story. Their differences are meaningless because of what separates both from the God "who lives in unapproachable light" (1 Timothy 6:16). Before the infinite, all finites are the same.[7]

THE GREATEST DESPAIR AND THE GREATEST HOPE

The first hope that the gospel brings to our misery is that while it's not good to be bad, it is good to know we're bad. The greatest misery is not to be miserable, but not to know we are miserable. "If you were blind, you would not be guilty of sin," Jesus said to the spiritual lepers of his day. "But now that you claim you can see, your guilt remains" (John 9:41). Knowledge of our despair is the first step toward the comfort of the gospel—and the deep, satisfying joy we seek.

Not to understand the enormity of sin is to miss the magnitude of grace. The gospel is a kind of antiphonal song sung back and forth between two choirs. One sings of human depravity and brokenness. The other answers with God's grace and our belovedness. The louder and more searingly the first choir sings, the stronger, more beautifully and joyfully the second sings. Where sin abounds, grace abounds much more (Romans 6:1). But to minimize sin is to minimize grace, and with it the gratitude and joy it produces.

The second step, according to the Catechism's summary of the gospel message, is to know "how I am set free from all my sins and misery." If it is true that "the wages of sin is death," it is also true that the "gift of God is eternal life in Christ Jesus our Lord" (Romans 6:23). The answer to our sin and misery is not trying harder to be what we can't. The answer is God's gift, expressed in the life, death and resurrection of Jesus Christ.

Paul wanted the Ephesian Christians to appreciate this, so he reminded them of what they were before God's grace. Walking with them through step one of joy, he wrote, "As for you, you were dead in your transgressions and sins, in which you used to live when you followed the ways of this world. . . . Gratifying the cravings of our sinful nature . . . like the rest, we were by nature objects of wrath" (Ephesians 2:1-4). Do you remember? he seems to be asking. This was you.

Now for step two of joy: "But because of his great love for us, God, who is rich in mercy, made us alive with Christ even when we were dead in transgressions—it is by grace you have been saved" (Ephesians 2:4-5). They were as helpless as dead people before God's grace came to them. How helpless is a dead person? Go to a cemetery and find out. Stand over a grave and encourage the person buried beneath you to walk. How's it going? Not so good? Now you can appreciate the stupendous miracle of grace that raises spiritually dead people and makes them alive in Christ—that makes *you* alive in Christ. Can you feel the gratitude and the joy begin to well up?

YOU'D BETTER BE VERY, VERY GRATEFUL

When Paul wrote to the Romans, again driving home the force of step two of joy, he wrote, "You see, at just the right time, when we were still powerless, Christ died for the ungodly. Very rarely will anyone die for a righteous man, though for a good man someone might possibly dare to die. But God demonstrates his own love for us in this: While we were still sinners, Christ died for us" (Romans 5:6-8).

Let me paraphrase. The chances of me giving my life for you are slim. (Please don't take it personally.) But—and it is a huge but—if you could convince me that your life was more important to the human race than mine, I might consider dying in your place. There would be a few provisos, however. One, I'd want you to witness my execution. Two, I'd want it videotaped. Three, I'd want you to promise in writing, on pain of your own death, to watch the videotape every day for the rest of your life. Four, I'd want you to promise to distribute the tape to everyone you know. In other words, I'd want you and as many others as possible to be very grateful.

Now hear Paul again: "But God demonstrates his own love for us in this: While we were still sinners, Christ died for us" (Romans 5:8). That means God loved us to the uttermost before we cared and whether or not we ever would care. There is nothing we can do to make him love us more—or less. God's love is so great, so free that he loved us as much as possible before we could respond in any way—before gratitude, with or without gratitude.

It is critical that we receive this life-transforming truth in the deepest and most tender region of our hearts. The deeper it goes, the deeper our joy will be. The spiritual dullness that comes with bland familiarity is deadly. It produces in us something like the attitude of the French philosopher and skeptic Voltaire. He is reputed to have mused, "I like to sin; God likes to forgive. It's a marvelous arrangement." That sentiment is a terrible and cheapening caricature of God's forgiveness. Grace does not come from an indulgent tolerance in the divine character; it comes at a great price—the blood of Christ his Son.

In his book *Written in Blood*, Robert Coleman tells a story of this kind of love on a human level. A little boy's sister was fatally ill and needed a blood transfusion. She had a disease he had recovered from two years earlier, and her only chance of survival was to receive antibodies that could help her fight the illness. Since he had the same rare blood type as his sister, the boy was the ideal donor.

"Would you give your blood to Mary?" the doctor asked.

That was a tough question. Johnny's lower lip trembled as he hesitated for a moment. Then he grinned and said, "Sure, for my sister."

Lying side by side, the brother and sister were wheeled into the hospital room. Johnny was strong and healthy; Mary was pale and thin. They didn't talk, but when their eyes met, Johnny smiled.

His smile faded as the nurse inserted the needle into his arm and his blood began to flow through the tube into his sister's body.

The room was silent until the ordeal was almost over. Then Johnny spoke. "Doctor, when do I die?"[8] The doctor was stunned to realize that the boy was prepared to make the ultimate sacrifice to save his sister.

Happily, he didn't have to. But God's Son did die to save us. Peter reminds us, "For you know that it was not with perishable things such as silver or gold that you were redeemed . . . but with the precious blood of Christ" (1 Peter 1:18-19). Significantly, Peter makes this statement just ten verses after he describes the Christian experience as one of "inexpressible and glorious joy" (1 Peter 1:8).

A Hallelujah from Head to Foot

Augustine described a Christian as "a hallelujah from head to foot." Sin and death are total, but salvation is victorious over them. Therefore the question implicit in the gospel is: Do I hear an amen? A thank you? How about a gospel song—or a dance?

Here is love, vast as the ocean,
Loving kindness as the flood,
When the Prince of Life, our ransom,
Shed for us his precious blood.
Who his love will not remember,
Who can cease to sing his praise?
He will never be forgotten
Throughout heaven's eternal days.

On the mount of crucifixion,
Fountains opened deep and wide,
Through the floodgates of God's mercy
Flowed a vast and gracious tide.

Grace and love, like mighty rivers,
Poured incessant from above,
And heaven's peace and perfect justice
Kissed a guilty world in love.[9]

Gratitude and joy are the most natural responses to the grace of God. They are step three in the Catechism's gospel summary: "how I am to thank God for such a deliverance." Joy is what you experience when you are grateful for the gospel and the abundant life that flows from it.

This view is present everywhere in the Bible. For Paul, the joyful life is lived always "in view of God's mercy" (Romans 12:1). Why should one be wholly devoted to God? In order to get salvation? Never; it can't be "gotten." It can only be received by faith, with gratitude. There is no motive possible other than humble gratitude. It is therefore "in view of God's mercy" that Paul urges his readers "to offer your bodies as living sacrifices, holy and pleasing to God" (Romans 12:1). Do this one thing—live in view of God's mercy—and everything will change. We will not conform to the pattern of the world around us, but be transformed by the renewing of our minds (Romans 12:2). Nothing will look the same again. Gratitude and joy will take over.

Even at its hardest, a life lived in view of God's mercy remains a pursuit of joy, an imitation of Christ, "who *for the joy* set before him endured the cross" (Hebrews 12:2, emphasis added). It's what keeps an aging apostle going after enduring, among many other things, eight floggings, a stoning in which he was left for dead, and a candid admission that he'd just as soon die and be with God than keep up the weary pace (2 Corinthians 11:24-25; Acts 14:19-20; Philippians 1:23). Paul testifies that it is Christ's love and joy that compels him to continue (2 Corinthians 5:14; Philippians 1:25-26).

OUR SPIRITUAL DNA

The Sermon on the Mount (Matthew 5—7) is the most exacting and rigorous ethical statement in history. For instance, Jesus says it's not enough to simply avoid the physical act of adultery; even to look at a woman lustfully is to do the deed (Matthew 5:27-30). Also, "You have heard that it was said, 'Love your neighbor and hate your enemy.' But I tell you: Love your enemies and pray for those who persecute you" (Matthew 5:43-44). Exacting and rigorous is putting it mildly.

However, at its core the sermon is liberating. Even as he tells us to do the exceedingly hard thing, to love our enemies, Jesus tells us why we must and can love our enemies: "In that way, you will be acting as true children of your Father in heaven" (Matthew 5:45 NLT). We must love this way because we belong to the God who has made us his children in Christ. This kind of love is more than a duty—it's in our spiritual genes. Earlier in the sermon Jesus says, "Let your good deeds shine out for all to see, so that everyone will praise your heavenly Father" (Matthew 5:16 NLT). Love like this is also our spiritual passion: we want to do good so others will come to feel about our Father as we do. We want to please him by moving others to praise him—that is, to be enthusiastically thankful for his goodness. As we are.

There is no greater honor we can give God than to live for him in this spirit. The chief end of humankind, according to the Westminster Shorter Catechism, is to glorify God and enjoy him forever. John Piper is right to add that the greatest way to glorify him *is* to enjoy him forever. God is most glorified when we are most satisfied in him.[10]

In my opinion, the finest picture of this glorious gospel outside the Bible is Charles Dickens's tale of Ebenezer Scrooge, a man incapable of joy. His story is the gospel in paraphrase. Scrooge is extremely rich, but he lives alone in barren squalor. He takes pleasure in nothing, hates almost everything and is indifferent to human suffering.

On Christmas Eve, Scrooge is visited by a series of ghosts who take him on a tumultuous journey of insight into his own character. They show him with jarring clarity how pain and disappointment have made him self-absorbed, bitter and callous. Love has been all around him, but he turned away from it. The ghost of Christmas future has the most shocking vision of all. In a desolate graveyard, the spirit's bony finger points Scrooge toward a headstone. Scrooge is wordlessly commanded to wipe the snow off and read the name carved on it. He knows the name will be his own. Weeping and shaking, Scrooge pleads with the spirit:

> Are these the shadows of the things that will be, or are they the
> shadows of the things that may be, only? . . . Men's courses will
> foreshadow certain ends . . . but if the course be departed from, the
> ends will change. Say it is thus with what you show me! . . . Hear
> me! I am not the man I was. . . . Oh tell me I may sponge away the
> writing on this stone![11]

That last sentence is the most wrenching of all. Can words etched in stone be wiped away with a sponge? Can the past be removed? Humanly speaking, it's impossible. And that is the human predicament. We are chained to our pasts, to things done and undone that cannot be changed. "What is twisted cannot be straightened; / what is lacking cannot be counted" (Ecclesiastes 1:15). The misdeeds of the past are like chains. Our guilt is carved in stone—or so it seems.

Scrooge awakens from his vision and discovers he is not dead. He still has time, the course can be departed from, the end may change, he is not the man he was. Grace is given! Joyful, he dances around his bedroom: "I'm as light as a feather, I'm as happy as an angel, I'm as merry as a schoolboy, I'm as giddy as a drunken man." And then, in the movie version of the story, the old man jumps up and down on his bed, falls backward and shouts, laughing, "Merry Christmas to everybody, and a happy New Year to the world!"[12] And it is said that from thenceforth nobody knew how to celebrate Christmas like Ebenezer Scrooge.

Ebenezer, significantly, is the biblical name for a pile of stones the Jews put up to remember an event of God's goodness and grace in their history. When Scrooge's stone is wiped clean, he lives the rest of his days gratefully and joyfully as a memorial stone of that event.

Dickens titled his tale "A Christmas Carol." A carol, according to the dictionary, is a song of joy and mirth, especially of the religious kind. To behold what God has done for us in Christ is to see ourselves as Scrooge saw himself in his desolation, and then generously and inexplicably be given a new life. It is to be made grateful, to sing a song of joy and mirth, and to know how to really celebrate, forever.

PART TWO

THE HABITS OF JOY

Joy is a gift of the Holy Spirit.

The Spirit is like the wind.

Habits of joy are the ways we

spread our sails.

5

INDISCRIMINATE THANKS

Rejoice in the Lord always. I will say it again: Rejoice!

PHILIPPIANS 4:4

Be joyful always; pray continually; give thanks in all circumstances,
for this is God's will for you in Christ Jesus.

1 THESSALONIANS 5:16-18

Thieves robbed Matthew Henry, the great eighteenth-century Bible scholar. Afterward he wrote in his diary, "Let me be thankful first because I was never robbed before; second, although they took my purse, they did not take my life; third, because, although they took my all, it was not much; and fourth, because it was I who was robbed, and not someone else."[1] It's hard to know what to make of this outlook. Was it the ruminations of an eighteenth-century Norman Vincent Peale? Or was there some wonderful power at work in this man?

His outlook was not unique. William Law, another eighteenth-century Christian thinker, took the same position:

> Would you know who is the greatest saint in the world? It is not he who prays most or fasts most, it is not he who gives most alms or is most eminent for temperance, chastity or justice; but it is he who is always thankful to God, who wills everything that God wills, who receives everything as an instance of God's goodness

and has a heart always ready to praise God for it. . . . Could you therefore work miracles, you could not do more for yourself than by this thankful spirit, for it . . . turns all that it touches into happiness.[2]

Both Henry and Law were strongly intent on obeying, to the literal letter, the command in Scripture to be indiscriminately thankful, to "rejoice in the Lord always" (Philippians 4:4). But they were doing much more than that. They were, in their obedience to the command of Scripture, engaging in a spiritual discipline, a habit of joy that is profoundly transforming.

AN ACT OF RECOVERY

There are three reasons why indiscriminate thanksgiving powerfully works joy in us. The first is that it is an act of recovery. According to the Bible, the core and origin of the human predicament is ingratitude. The bitter root of every other evil is pride that will not give credit where it is due. Everything wrong with us starts here: "For although they knew God, they neither glorified him as God nor gave thanks to him, but their thinking became futile and their foolish hearts were darkened" (Romans 1:21). The darkness of ingratitude is protean in its manifestations—showing itself as murder, lust, greed, sexual perversion, envy, deceit, malice, callousness and every other form of human sin (see Romans 1:18-25).

What is it about ingratitude that is so fundamentally and devastatingly evil? It is the ultimate dismissal of God—and of all that is good, for all that is good is of God. It is the deepest form of hatred, the most radical of snubs. Not to thank God is to act as though he didn't exist or didn't matter. Samuel Johnson called gratitude a "species of justice" because to give thanks is to recognize the fundamental truth of our existence: that all we are and have comes from God, that it is he who made us, and it is in him that "we live and move and have our being" (Acts 17:28). What could be more perverse and inverted than to ignore this essential truth? But that is precisely what ingratitude does. Every other perversity starts here.

To practice the discipline of gratitude is to shine light into the heart of our darkness. Certainly we are not saved by gratitude; we are saved only by God's grace and mercy. But since Jesus died for our sins, all of which are the result of ingratitude, to practice gratitude is to cooperate with this grace. Paul urged the Philippian Christians to "continue to work out your salvation with fear and trembling, for it is God who works in you to will and to act according to his good purpose" (Philippians 2:12-13). In this sense, gratitude is a powerful act of recovery.

BEHAVING LIKE A CUSTOMER IN A WELL-RUN HOTEL

It's significant that Paul's very next exhortation is to be grateful in a particular way, to "do everything without complaining or arguing" (Philippians 2:14). A spirit of complaint doesn't ignore God, it just accuses him of mismanagement. It leads us to live in God's world like a dissatisfied customer in a well-run hotel.

A spirit of complaining is subtly poisonous because it is often regarded as a relatively harmless, almost acceptable peccadillo in the Christian life. Maybe this is because it is so easy to complain. Unlike the "big sins" of adultery, theft and murder, which require some determination and effort to commit, all one has to do is open one's mouth. God takes no such view. A spirit of complaint caused God to stall the Israelites in the wilderness for forty years, and he denied a whole generation entry into the land of promise. They were tired, they were hungry, they were afraid, and it was all God's fault, they thought (see Exodus 17 and Numbers 20). At places subsequently named for their complaining—Massah, "the place of testing," and Meribah, "the place of arguing"—the Israelites grumbled their way into a hole they never got out of. To this day, the result of their complaining—which was basically ingratitude—is a warning of the destruction that comes when God is accused of mismanagement. Psalm 95 has been read, recited, prayed and sung by Israel and the church for centuries:

Come, let us bow down in worship,
let us kneel before the LORD our Maker;

for he is our God
    and we are the people of his pasture,
    the flock under his care. (vv. 6-7)

God is in charge, says the psalm. He's not detached; he really cares for us—after all, he is our Maker; he is our God, we are his people; we are the sheep of his pasture. Everything he does he does in perfect love, wisdom and power. However, if we refuse to be grateful and slide down the slippery slope of complaint, consequences await us:

Today, if you hear his voice,
    do not harden your hearts as you did at Meribah,
    as you did that day at Massah in the desert,
where your fathers tested and tried me,
    though they had seen what I did.
For forty years I was angry with that generation;
    I said, "They are a people whose hearts go astray,
    and they have not known my ways."
So I declared on oath in my anger,
    "They shall never enter my rest." (Psalm 95:7-11)

Ungrateful complaint was the cause of a whole generation's failure to know God's best. They whined themselves into frustration and the grave. Their inheritance was consumed in peevishness. Complaint is a devastating thing.

COMPLAINING TO GOD OR ABOUT GOD?

A thoughtful reader may wonder, but what about all those psalms that complain to God—like Psalm 88?

You have put me in the lowest pit,
    in the darkest depths.
Your wrath lies heavily upon me;
    you have overwhelmed me with all your waves.
You have taken from me my closest friends
    and have made me repulsive to them.

> I am confined and cannot escape;
>> my eyes are dim with grief. (Psalm 88:6-9)

Is it sinful to vent this way to the Lord? Not at all. The difference between prayers of honest complaint and the kind of thing that destroyed a generation of Israel is in the prepositions. True prayer complains *to* God. Mere griping complains *about* God. There is a world of difference: when you voice to God your complaint, it becomes a bridge to a deeper relationship. When you voice it to others, it becomes a wedge in the relationship. Prayers of complaint end in question marks; grumbling ends in exclamation points.[3] The former are open-ended, demonstrate a teachable spirit and can lead to praise; the latter are shut up in themselves, hardened to any new insight and end in bitterness.

Thomas Merton wrote vividly of the importance of uncomplaining gratitude:

> There is no neutrality between gratitude and ingratitude. Those who are not grateful soon begin to complain of everything. Those who do not love, hate. In the spiritual life there is no such thing as an indifference to love or hate. That is why tepidity (which seems to be indifferent) is so detestable. It is hate disguised as love. Tepidity, in which the soul is neither "hot nor cold"—neither frankly loves nor frankly hates—is a state in which one rejects God and rejects the will of God while maintaining an exterior pretense of loving him in order to stay out of trouble and save one's supposed self-respect. To be grateful is to recognize the love of God in everything. Every breath we draw is a gift of his love, every moment of existence is a gift of grace, for it brings with it immense graces from him. Gratitude takes nothing for granted, is never unresponsive, is constantly awakening to new wonder and to praise of the goodness of God. For the grateful man knows that God is good, not by hearsay but by experience.[4]

To give thanks liberally, indiscriminately, even outrageously is to know not only peace, but a joy that "transcends all understanding" (Philippians 4:7).

AN ACT OF HOPE

Second, the discipline of giving thanks in all circumstances is an act of hope. When we give thanks no matter what, we act on the premise that the future will turn out perfectly. The next moment may be dreadful, even the next decade or two, but he who holds the last hour has assured us that everything will be glorious in the end. When we give thanks we rejoice in that hope, just as the Bible says:

> And we rejoice in the hope of the glory of God. Not only so, but we also rejoice in our sufferings, because we know that suffering produces perseverance; perseverance, character; and character, hope. And hope does not disappoint us, because God has poured out his love into our hearts by the Holy Spirit, whom he has given us. (Romans 5:2-5)

Hope is the firm confidence that nothing can separate us from God's love, and "that our present sufferings are not worth comparing with the glory that will be revealed in us" (Romans 8:18). With that conviction, we can rejoice in every situation and give indiscriminate thanks. Really, it's a kind of reality check.

Plato's famous cave analogy has helped me think about this. Suppose a man is born in a cave and spends his entire life tied to a post, facing the wall at the rear of the cave. He cannot look to the right or the left, only forward. The light from outside shines on the wall he faces. Occasionally people and animals walk by the cave's entrance and cast shadows on the wall. These shadows and the dim light are the only reality he knows. A world outside the cave, made of color and three dimensions, would be incomprehensible to him.

But what if a mirror were held up to him in which he could glimpse the world outside? Everything would change. He would see the shadows in the larger context and deeper reality of a world of depth and color. That's what hope is to the shadows of this life: the larger context and deeper reality of God's faithful love to be revealed in the future. Or, to change the metaphor, "Hope is the music of the future," wrote Rubem Alves. "Faith is to dance to it."[5]

Indiscriminate thanksgiving rejoices in what is seen in the mirror. It exults in a future more real and permanent than the present. That's what Paul meant when he wrote, "Therefore we do not lose heart. Though outwardly we are wasting away, yet inwardly we are being renewed day by day. For our light and momentary troubles are achieving for us an eternal glory that far outweighs them all. So we fix our eyes not on what is seen, but on what is unseen. For what is seen is temporary, but what is unseen is eternal" (2 Corinthians 4:16-18).

For the Christian, whatever heaviness the present may contain is as light as a feather compared to the weight of future glory. To give thanks no matter what is to open a little window in the present darkness to let in the light of the glory of the world to come.

Late one evening I was listening to the radio while driving home from a speaking engagement. The station was playing one popular song after another from 1966, the last year I was in college. Music can be quite evocative of memory; nostalgia was oozing out of my pores as I sang along. I remembered my roommates—what a great bunch of guys. I remembered my football teammates—what fun we had. The four years of college I stretched into six seemed to be the best years of my life as I sang. In my mind I had been a carefree and callow young buck, innocent and unafraid.

Then I remembered how miserable I was my senior year. The girl I loved had jilted me; I had almost gotten into a fistfight with one of my roommates; I was tired of school, uncertain of my calling and afraid of the future. I thought of how good my life had been since then. I murmured gratitude to God for the woman I married, the kids we'd had together, the work he had graciously given me to do and the great friends I had. All my 1966 fears had since been unmasked as frauds. Then I thought of what a waste it had been to be so anxious and fearful back in college. Had I only known how well my life would turn out, I could have relaxed and enjoyed my senior year. I fantasized, wouldn't it be wonderful to live that year again, knowing what I know now? *Too bad I can't,* I thought; what a loss. But then something glorious occurred to me: I can live from now on knowing that my life is going to turn out fine. I can let

God's future dictate the terms of the present. I can give thanks indiscriminately as an act of hope, acting as though everything God promised
about the future is true. Because it is.

AN ACT OF DEFIANCE

Third, this kind of hopeful, indiscriminate gratitude can be an act of joyful defiance. There are bullies in life, things huge and terrifying, intimi-
dating and overwhelming: death, an unhappy lab report, a job loss, a
professional failure, a bad investment. They are bigger and meaner than
we are, and they use their threatening nature to push us around and hold
us down. However, we can stand up straight, look these punks in the eye
and give thanks; in doing this we stand on a rock they can never shake.
They may be more than we can handle in our own power, but to give
thanks is to triumph nevertheless. The joy of the Lord then becomes our
strength indeed (Nehemiah 8:10).

It was God's defiant "Nevertheless!" that triumphed over our sin and
guilt and saved us, once and for all, from death and the power of the devil.
Though we deserved the bad thing, we got the good thing in Christ nevertheless. His blood was innocent, but he shed it for our sins nevertheless.
That's how determined God was to be both just and the one who justifies
the unrighteous (Romans 3:26). God's "Nevertheless!" spoken on the cross
is a sovereignly holy and defiant act.

If God's grace is defiant, then our gratitude should also be defiant. If
God refused to let our guilt be the final word, then we too should refuse
to let any of life's bullies have the final word. Nothing should ever rob us
of our joy because nothing should be given the power to take away our
sense of gratitude for God's defiant grace.

I have a friend who loves to speak of "dancing on the Egyptian side
of the Red Sea." He is referring to the story in Exodus when Israel was
backed up against the Red Sea, hemmed in on the left and right by
mountains and facing a murderous Egyptian army bearing down on
them from the desert. They were in a panic; then Moses spoke to them:
"Do not be afraid. Stand firm and you will see the deliverance the LORD
will bring you today. The Egyptians you see today you will never see

again. The LORD will fight for you; you need only to be still" (Exodus 14:13-14). Things turned out great, and God did just as Moses said he would. The waters of the sea miraculously parted, the Egyptian army drowned when the waters came back together, and Israel danced joyously on the other side.

But how glorious, how defiantly and exquisitely joyous would it have been if they had believed God and danced on the Egyptian side of the Red Sea? The Egyptian bullies would have been doubly defeated, God doubly glorified, and their joy doubly intensified. That is the power of indiscriminate thanks.

SINGING LIKE A BLACK LADY

In chapter two I mentioned my friend Bishop Roderick Caesar and his wonderful church, the Bethel Gospel Tabernacle. If ever a people's worship was danced and sung to the music of the future, theirs is. My seven-year-old daughter, Mary, was with us on a Sunday I preached there, and she was very impressed by what she saw and heard. She listened carefully as these godly African Americans shared their prayer concerns. Jamaica Queens can be a dangerous place to raise children, so some of the prayers were for protection for their kids against gangs and guns and drugs at school. Mary's eyes grew big and she became still as she listened. Then she participated in a joyous service of song—and dance!—quite unlike anything she had ever seen as the child of a Presbyterian pastor.

A few weeks later my wife, Lauretta, came home a little late, fifteen minutes after Mary was to be home from school. As Lauretta walked up to the door she heard Mary inside, singing loudly and boisterously. When Lauretta opened the door, Mary whirled around, ran to her mom and hugged her. She had been scared to be home alone, she said. The lower level of our house was especially frightening; it was dark down there and who knew what might be lurking in the shadows? So she had stood at the top of the steps and sung into the darkness. Lauretta asked her why she had sung in that particular style. Mary answered, "I was scared, so I started singing like a black lady!"

She had learned something that Sunday in Jamaica Queens that I hope she will carry with her the rest of her life: when the present is terrifying, she can sing defiantly into the darkness because the future's going to be wonderful!

FOR EVERYTHING?

Indiscriminate thanksgiving works powerfully to produce the unique joy that comes from defying life's bullies. To give thanks in all things is a radical and joyous act (1 Thessalonians 5:16-18). When we speak our "nevertheless," we hear God's more clearly. But what about Paul's even more radical command to give thanks *for* all things (Ephesians 5:20)? What a difference a preposition makes! Can we really say thank you to God not only in everything but for everything? Can we thank God for evil? Should we thank God for evil?

Some reference points may be helpful here. One, we should be careful not to make too much of one line of Scripture. The Bible is its own best interpreter. This verse should be read in the light of other passages that assure us God is never the author of evil. Whatever conclusions we draw from one part of Scripture should be influenced by all the rest.

Two, the world lives under God's judgment. Because of sin—the sin not only of the first humans, but yours and mine also—the creation has been "subjected to frustration." This frustration was "not by its own choice, but by the will of the one who subjected it" (Romans 8:20; see also Genesis 3:17-19). The one who brought that frustration was God. Whatever chaos and brokenness, whatever random acts of violence we may experience, it is ultimately the result of our own sin and the righteous judgment of a holy God.

If I am the victim of a robbery tomorrow, I may not deserve that specific act of injustice. And it would be a mistake to simplistically say it was God's will. But I do deserve the kind of world where things like that can happen. In this sense, then, should we thank God that we suffer under his judgment? I think we should, for God would not be God or good if we did not suffer. It is ultimately the hard edge of his justice when so-called bad things happen to so-called good people. It is an act of great humility to recognize this.

Three, the Romans text adds that God subjected this world to frustration "in hope that the creation itself will be liberated from its bondage to decay and brought into the glorious freedom of the children of God" (Romans 8:20-21). The final word is not judgment, but hope. God's judgment was for the sake of hope. The evil of this world must somehow therefore finally serve God's good purposes. So we read later, "And we know that in all things God works for the good of those who love him, who have been called according to his purpose" (Romans 8:28). Whatever frustration we now experience will be swallowed up in freedom one day. God's holy and loving purposes will triumph not in spite of the frustration and futility of this world, but through it.

Four, the best and clearest perspective for this challenging verse comes from another verse: "For God so loved the world that he gave his one and only Son, that whoever believes in him shall not perish but have eternal life" (John 3:16). God is passionate for the fulfillment of hope in this broken world. He willed the frustration, but he also wills the redemption, at great cost. It cost him his own Son. Even as we thank God for his justice, we can weep knowing he has wept also. Go to Gethsemane and see (Matthew 26:34-46). God's love kisses his justice every time the world groans under his judgment. For that we can thank him.

To thank God for all things is to stand on a high precipice and see the beginning and the end. It is not for the faint of heart. It is strong medicine but good medicine, and it is the only cure for our narcissism. It gave Job the strength to worship and pray even when he lost all his children. "Naked I came from my mother's womb, / and naked I will depart. / The LORD gave and the LORD has taken away; / may the name of the LORD be praised" (Job 1:21). He didn't complain that they were taken from him; he was grateful that he had them at all. Whatever confusion and perplexity we experience, this truth remains: "Let God be true, and every man [and situation and circumstance] a liar" (Romans 3:4).

ORGANS OF PERCEPTION

Gratitude and joy are organs of perception; we don't see in order to give thanks and rejoice, we give thanks and rejoice in order to see. Do you

see no reason to be joyful and grateful? Rejoice and give thanks so you
will! The truth of our human limitation is that we never see all there is,
whether of evil or good. We never have all the information. But if God is
everything he claims to be, if he indeed is always working for the good
of those who love him (Romans 8:28), then we have every reason to be
disposed toward gratitude even when our eyes see only the terrible.

God cannot be pleased without faith (Hebrews 11:6), so to exercise
faith by rejoicing and giving thanks regardless of circumstances is pleasing to him. The discipline of thanksgiving involves thanking God for
what we see, and when we see nothing to thank him for, then thanking
him for what we do not see. Virginia Owens writes,

> For if you go poking about the world, intent on keeping the candle
> of consciousness blazing, you must be ready to give thanks at all
> times. Discrimination is not allowed. The flame cannot gutter and
> fail when a cold wind whistles throughout the house. Thanksgiv-
> ing, thanksgiving. All must be thanksgiving. . . . Thanksgiving is
> not a task to be taken lightly. It is not for dilettantes or aesthetes.
> One does not dabble in praise for one's own amusement, nor train
> the intellect and develop perceptual skills to add to his repertoire.
> We are not thinking about the world as a free course in art appre-
> ciation. No. Thanksgiving is not the result of perception; thanks-
> giving is the access to perception.[6]

Three images help us to understand these truths. The first is Isaiah's
vision of the city of God. Its walls are called Salvation, and its gates are
named Praise (Isaiah 60:18). To be with God is to be liberated, saved
from sin and death. To enter the city of God is to come through gates of
praise—gratitude for the grace he has given in this salvation. Joy in his
presence and eternal pleasures at his right hand are its great reward
(Psalm 16:11). A life of indiscriminate thanks is part of our pilgrimage
to that city.

The second image is of an elixir, a stone that medieval alchemists believed would turn all it touched to gold. Such a stone was never found,
but the poet George Herbert believed in a spiritual elixir—a sense of

God's presence in all things. He prayed,

> Teach me, my God and King,
> In all things Thee to see,
> And what I do in any thing
> To do it as for Thee. . . .
>
> This is the famous stone
> That turneth all to gold;
> For that which God doth touch and own
> Cannot for less be told.[7]

Indiscriminate gratitude is perhaps the chief way we recognize God's presence in all things. As William Law put it, "Could you therefore work miracles, you could not do more for yourself than by this thankful spirit, for it . . . turns all that it touches into happiness."[8]

The third image is of the Amazon River, the biggest river in the world. Its volume is greater than the Yangtze, Mississippi and Nile combined. In the early days of European exploration, ships would sometimes be caught in the doldrums for days in the Amazon's ninety-mile-wide mouth, thinking they were still far out to sea. Supplies would run low, water would be gone, and sailors would die of thirst. When South American natives canoed out to their ships, the frantic sailors would ask where to find fresh water. The natives would laugh and point to the water beneath them. The sailors had no idea of the vast quantities of refreshment all around them. The same is true of us. The discipline of indiscriminate thanks, a habit of joy, opens our eyes to the abundance of God's grace all around us.

～ 6 ～

KNOWLEDGE
TOO WONDERFUL

My God, Thou art all love:
Not one poor minute 'scapes Thy breast,
But brings a favor from above;
And in this love, more than in bed I rest.

GEORGE HERBERT

On display at the Museum of Modern Art in New York City is a sculpture of a hand by French sculptor Auguste Rodin. It was one of his favorites, a piece that he and his students often duplicated. Emerging from its palm are what appear to be the clay figures of a man and a woman. He titled the piece *The Hand of God*. Picture that hand, and absorb this transforming truth: Every moment of your life you have been held by a hand—whether or not you are aware of it, and whether or not you care.

Joy is what we experience when we are grateful for the grace given us. If there is no joy, there must be a breakdown somewhere between the "grace" and the "grateful." Maybe we struggle to see the grace surrounding us, the hand holding us, the love that has known us all our life. How can we be grateful for a grace we haven't seen?

The secret is that God always makes the first move. He's always there ahead of us. "We love because he first loved us" (1 John 4:19). John Wesley called this God's "prevenient grace." It's an archaic word, *prevenient,* but a good one. It means that God is eternally and lovingly "pre"—before us, ahead of us. If God had not first been looking for us, we could never have found him. Had God not first grasped our hand, we could never hold his. Had God not first opened our eyes, we could never see him. Even our prayers are possible because of him. "Our prayer," writes Peter Taylor Forsyth, "is the answer to God's."[1] God holds us by his initiative, anticipating and seeking us in love.

HELD BY HIS KNOWLEDGE

The Bible is especially interested in how God holds us by knowing us. Historically, many theologians have tended to think of God's knowledge as pure intellect, awesome only in its comprehensiveness. He is omniscient, they say. He knows all there is to know, all that was and is and will be. These thinkers are so impressed with God's intellect, and by extension their own as students of that intellect, that given the choice between going to heaven or hearing a lecture about heaven, some have suggested they would choose the lecture.

This intellect is impressive, to be sure. Contrast his knowledge with ours. Ours is limited and successive. That is, we must learn one thing, then another, building knowledge block upon knowledge block. God's knowledge, however, is total and simultaneous. He knows everything there is to know instantaneously. Moreover, our knowledge is discursive; we must be taught what we know. God's is innate and intuitive—he just knows.

But if God's knowledge were strictly informational, it would be terrifying to ponder. It would be like what Revolutionary War hero Marquis de Lafayette experienced when he was locked in solitary confinement as a prisoner of war for several years. He never saw another human being, only the eye of a guard staring at him through a hole drilled in the door of his cell. Terrifying, that eye, he later reported. It stripped him bare, paralyzing him with its cold scrutiny. God's knowledge of us can feel that way. Indeed, "Nothing in all creation is hidden from God's sight. Everything is uncovered and laid bare before the eyes of him to whom we must give account" (Hebrews 4:13).

THE KNOWLEDGE OF A LOVER

But that's not the emphasis of Scripture. God is not a celestial computer that crunches human data for divine analysis. His knowledge holds us not through fright but through love. Over and over again, the Bible presents a beautiful picture of God knowing us the way a husband knows his wife. And that knowledge is anything but mere cognition. When Adam knew his wife, what happened? She got pregnant! Thomas Howard writes:

> This is a piquant irony. Here we are, with all our high notions of ourselves as intellectual and spiritual beings, and the most profound form of knowledge for us is a plain business of skin on skin. It is humiliating. When two members of this godlike, cerebral species approach the heights of communion between themselves, what do they do? Think? Speculate? Meditate? No, they take off their clothes. Do they want to get their brains together? No. It is the most appalling of ironies: Their search for union takes them quite literally in a direction away from where their brains are.[2]

God's knowledge of us is intimate, visceral, personal—an intercourse of which the earthly form is but a shadow. It speaks of union and self-giving. Isaiah says, "As a bridegroom rejoices over his bride, / so will your God rejoice over you" (Isaiah 62:5).

Therefore, in Psalm 139, God's knowledge is cause for wonder and delight:

> O LORD, you have searched me
>   and you know me.
> You know when I sit and when I rise;
>   you perceive my thoughts from afar.
> You discern my going out and my lying down;
>   you are familiar with all my ways.
> Before a word is on my tongue
>   you know it completely, O LORD.
> You hem me in—behind and before;
>   you have laid your hand upon me. (vv. 1-5)

David, the author, knows this is a lover's knowledge, not an inquisitor's, so he rhapsodizes: "Such knowledge is too wonderful for me, / too lofty for me to attain" (Psalm 139:6).

DO YOU KNOW SOMEONE WHO KNOWS YOU LIKE THAT?

Do you know someone who has loved you so long and so well that he or she can anticipate your next word, your next move? You're blessed if you do. You're delighted. And you're held by that love. You've been loved a little bit like God loves.

It's this intimate knowledge that makes confession of sin possible and bearable. God knows us. When we confess the evil we have done, he doesn't gasp and say, "Really? I had no idea!" He knows already and has been waiting for us to say we know too. And he loves us just as much before we confess as he does after. The thing that changes is not the amount of information God has but our relationship with him; in confession a wall becomes a door.

I have a picture of Jesus hanging in my home. Sometimes when we have guests, we place a table beneath it and load it up with good things to eat. That way, everyone who comes over for a snack gets a look at Jesus too—and a look from Jesus. In the picture he's laughing with affection and delight. It's really more of a smile than a laugh. He seems to be saying, "I know your foolishness and folly. I know everything about you, and I have every right to laugh at you—with scorn. But I'm not going to laugh at you, I'm going to laugh with you." His laugh makes me think of the way my wife looks at me.

This is the kind of knowledge and love God holds us with.

HELD BY HIS GRACIOUS PRESENCE

We are held also by God's presence. The cold theological term for this is *omnipresence*—the fact that all of God is always everywhere. Crawl into a cave in the bottom of the Grand Canyon and he's as much there as he is on top of Mount Everest, or under my desk. A girl was asked by her Sunday school teacher, "How do we know there is only one God?" The teacher expected her to answer, "Because the Bible says so." Instead the girl answered, "Because he's so big. He fills up everything, so there's no room for another god." Precisely!

This, of course, is cause for us to be sober. "'Am I only a God nearby,' / declares the LORD, / 'and not a God far away? Can anyone hide in secret places / so that I cannot see him?' declares the LORD. 'Do not I fill heaven and earth?' declares the LORD" (Jeremiah 23:23-24). There's no escaping him.

But as with his knowledge, God's immensity is conditioned by his grace. God is present everywhere—not against us, but for us. David asks a rhetorical question: "Where can I go from your Spirit? / Where can I flee from your presence?" (Psalm 139:7). He then responds by posing a series of what the poet Shel Silverstein calls the "whatifs," the worries that can nag at the edge of our consciousness, depriving us of our sleep and our peace of mind. The word *if* appears five times in the next five verses, covering some of the eventualities and exigencies of the possibilities of life apart from God's presence. None of them are sufficient cause for him to worry. No matter where he goes, God is there for him.

> If I go up to the heavens, you are there;
>> if I make my bed in the depths, you are there.
> If I rise on the wings of the dawn,
>> if I settle on the far side of the sea,
> even there your hand will guide me,
>> your right hand will hold me fast.
> If I say, "Surely the darkness will hide me
>> and the light become night around me,"
> even the darkness will not be dark to you;
>> the night will shine like the day,
>> for darkness is as light to you. (Psalm 139:8-12)

Each of us has a "whatif" list, including things like cancer, joblessness, loneliness, rejection, death, eternity—all the experiences we can imagine in this life and the next. But God is there, as David said, and as Paul affirmed also with his own "whatif" list: "For I am convinced that neither death nor life, neither angels nor demons, neither the present nor the future, nor any powers, neither height nor depth, nor anything else in all creation, will be able to separate us from the love of God that is in Christ Jesus our Lord" (Romans 8:38-39).

The famous astronomer Henry Norris Russell was lecturing at Princeton. A woman approached him after the lecture and said, "Dr. Russell, you've lectured on the Milky Way. You've made us aware of how big the universe is and how tiny the Earth is." Then she asked incredulously, "Can we believe that there is a God who would be interested in us?" Dr. Russell answered, "It depends entirely on how big a God you believe in."

HE'S IN HERE, HE'S OUT THERE, HE'S EVERYWHERE I CAN BE

The flipside of the immensity of God's gracious presence is the smallness of the spaces he wishes to occupy. I became a Christian as a child of nine in a child evangelism class held by a little old lady named Mrs. Dalton. She bribed us each week, promising a free Popsicle if we showed up and stayed. For a while that was the only reason my buddies and I went.

But over time, her message began to get through. No matter what Bible story she told, she always ended by showing us a picture of a red heart with a door on which Christ was knocking. She pointed out that the door had no knob on the outside, that it could be opened only from the inside. Then she would quote Revelation 3:20: "Here I am! I stand at the door and knock. If anyone hears my voice and opens the door, I will come in and eat with him, and he with me." That was Jesus speaking, she explained. The heart was ours, she said. So was the choice. Would we open the door and let him live with us forever?

I thought about it for a while, weighing the costs and benefits. With Jesus living in me she said I would go to heaven when I died. Without him there I would go to hell. I wasn't too smart, so even with those alternatives I thought quite a while about the matter. But one day I did decide to ask him in and knelt and prayed with my sister and Mrs. Dalton. I pictured a little Jesus coming through a little door into my heart and sitting down at a little table to eat with me. It felt good to think he was there inside—somehow even better than the promise of heaven over hell. I was held that day by his presence, and I have been ever since.

Since then I have read through the Bible several times, been to college and graduate school in theology, preached hundreds of sermons, written four books, contributed to many others and published scores of articles. I have thought long and hard about the mysteries of faith. But the little Jesus at the little table notwithstanding, I really can't improve much on the theology I learned that afternoon in 1951. He's in here; he's out there; he's everywhere I can be. And he holds me.

TWENTY-EIGHT THOUSAND POUNDS AT BIRTH?

His knowledge and his presence: with these the hand of God holds us. But he comes even closer. He holds us as he makes us. For David this is the greatest wonder of all. What's involved is not mere paternity, but God's loving, intimate creativity, which he pours into the process of fashioning one human being.

> For you created my inmost being;
>> you knit me together in my mother's womb.
> I praise you because I am fearfully and wonderfully made;
>> your works are wonderful,
>> I know that full well.
> My frame was not hidden from you
>> when I was made in the secret place.
> When I was woven together in the depths of the earth,
>> your eyes saw my unformed body. (Psalm 139:13-16)

God was there at the very beginning, in the softest, tiniest and darkest place—David's mother's womb—at work making him who he was.

Until recently, science knew next to nothing of the staggering scope of embryonic development in the first two weeks of life. So much is going on at this stage that according to Dr. Bernard Nathanson, if we continued to develop throughout gestation at the same rate as those first two weeks, we would weigh twenty-eight thousand pounds at birth! That's how fast the rate of cell division is. Add to this tumultuous multiplication process the intricate neurological and chemical organization taking place, and the picture is breathtaking. Life forces that translate into the ability to hit a baseball and cowlicks and the sound of a person's laugh are programmed into place.

In magnitude and complexity, it is a spectacle even greater than a tsunami or the transformation of winter into spring. The first two weeks of life are the most important in human development, which demolishes every logical argument for abortion. But the real glory and mystery is that all of this takes place on a microscopic scale. The grandest, most awesome stage of human life is virtually invisible. And God is there doing it all—knitting us together, intimately holding us.

WHAT MUSIC IT WOULD BE

There's more. But here the way God holds us becomes so difficult to fathom that it can cause either joy or consternation, depending on our circumstances. "All the days ordained for me / were written in your book / before one of them came to be" (Psalm 139:16). God made us and determined our experiences. How can we get our minds around that?

Here I think we do better with poets than with analytic philosophers and theologians. George Herbert spoke of this mystery in a long poem he aptly titled "Providence." He wants, as he puts it, to praise God that "all things have their will, yet none but Thine." Somehow we are free, yet God sovereignly manages to be in control, determining all that comes to us.

But events and experiences come to us in different ways. Some things happen by command, says Herbert; they are explicitly willed by God. Others occur with God's permission—he does not directly will these things but allows them within his grand purpose for us. In this way God is like a musician playing a guitar (or lute, as would have been the case for Herbert). We are the instrument played. His commanded will is his right hand, striking the strings of the instrument. His permitted will is his left hand, taking the resonance of the strings and making them sound the note that he, the musician, desires. The right hand determines what happens; the left hand responds to what is permitted.

For either Thy command or Thy permission
Lay hands on all; they are Thy right and left:

The first puts on with speed and expedition;
The other curbs Sin's stealing pace and theft.[3]

Of course no metaphor or poem explains how this is actually possible. The Bible doesn't either. But Herbert does describe how God is making music of our lives, if we could but hear it. "And we know that in all things God works for the good of those who love him, who have been called according to his purpose" (Romans 8:28). Nothing escapes God's command or permission.

All must appear,
And be disposed, and dressed, and tuned by Thee,
Who sweetly temperest all. If we could hear
Thy skill and art, what music it would be![4]

DANCING TO THE MUSIC IN HAHA

Our responsibility is to listen gratefully and expectantly for the music in our lives. This is what I try to do when I counsel with someone. I don't attempt to be a psychotherapist, and I'm sparing with answers and solutions. I've learned over the years that when a person in deep distress is crying out, "Why?" she isn't really asking a question, she's expressing grief and pain. Besides, we're like children; our ability to ask questions is greater than our ability to hear and understand answers. And for many of us, the answer to one question leads to yet another question and another and another. God never gives us the details of the score he has written for us—just a few bars for us to hum, if we will listen. To hope in God is not only to be able to hear that music, but to dance to it.[5]

A few years ago I received a letter from a couple my family loves. Extremely bright, this couple has devoted their lives and their keen minds to learning the language of a people group in a village called Haha (!) in Papua. They are teaching the people to read and write in their own language, and translating the Bible so they can eventually grow in the grace and knowledge of Jesus Christ—all while raising four children.

Among the hardships they endure is separation from friends and family for long periods of time. The wife's father, a beloved professor of literature, died of cancer while they were away. Their letter is a study in what it means to listen for the music of grace:

> On May 17 my dad died, preceding us to the Father's arms. Epis-
> copal priest, teacher of literature, scholar, worshiper of God, be-
> loved through life, he is sorely missed by us who are left behind.
> We look forward with longing to the day we will meet again. Al-
> ready in Haha when the news arrived by radio, we decided to stay,
> learning the sorrow of being far from home at such a time. In Haha,
> very few people our age have living parents. Death takes its toll
> early through disease and a very poor diet. All of our friends there
> know death intimately and shared our grief as they recalled their
> own. However, my mother and brother made plans to visit, and
> now in mid-July they came for a month's visit, giving us a time of
> comfort and completion regarding Dad's death.
>
> Give thanks with us for the following: The birth of our baby in
> July; Dad's death, as this too is from His loving hand; our new con-
> tacts; whatever God is planning for our future; the visit of my
> mother and brother; the progress of language study.

It's all one song for these people: a baby's birth, a father's death, doing God's work. There's music to be heard amid the noise and confusion be-cause of the God who holds them.

My friend, there is a hand holding you too, and it has been all your life—whether or not you know it, and whether or not you even care. But God wants you to know it. He wants you to reach out your hand and clasp his.

Be Dazzled

How do we do that? David gives some clues in the great psalm that has been popping up throughout this chapter. He says, in effect, that we should allow ourselves to be dazzled, to be filled with wonder. "Such knowledge is too wonderful for me, / too lofty for me to attain. . . . How precious to me are your thoughts, O God! / How vast is the sum of them!" (Psalm 139:6, 17).

Have you seen a child opening a gift at Christmas, clapping his hands and jumping up and down with delight? That's the emotion here. This is too wonderful, too lofty, too precious! I can hardly bear it!

We need to allow ourselves to be dazzled, to be wonder-full.[6]

Being dazzled means being humbled by what we know. The paradox is that as we are humbled, we will be exalted by the God who holds us. It works something like this: When my son Joel was twelve years old, we hiked into the Grand Canyon along with a close friend. The canyon is my favorite spot on earth, a place I never tire of staring at in wonder. On our last night we were sitting on the edge of the canyon watching the sun go down as we munched on summer sausage, cheese and crackers. The play of evening light on the canyon, the majestic changing of colors, was like a visual fugue. Our conversation turned from the arduous hike earlier that day to deeper things. We spoke quietly of God and creation and the kind of girl Joel ought to marry someday. I was intensely aware of how much I loved this wonder of a son. His profile was outlined against the glories of the canyon and the sunset. How precious to me are your thoughts, O God!

Pointing toward the canyon, Joel turned and said to my friend and me, "There's no place on earth that shows more of God's glory than this place!"

Ah! The perfect moment to say what had been welling up in my breast. I said, "There is, Joel. There is something that shows God's glory even better than this."

His eyes flashed, ready to debate the point. "Where, Dad?"

"Right here, buddy," I said, pointing at him. "This whole canyon doesn't add up to you. There is no canyon or river or mountain or ocean that better shows the majesty of God than you, or any other human being."

You, my friend, are grander than the Grand Canyon. You were knit together by the hand of God, and apart from Jesus Christ, you are his most amazing grace. To see yourself in this way is to be humbled and dazzled by the God who made you. Thank God for yourself and for the mystery and depth of your neighbor. Look at yourself in the mirror and say out loud to God, "I praise you for I am fearfully and wonderfully made. Good work, Lord."

Another book with a good title is *God Don't Make No Junk*. Bad grammar, but who cares? God doesn't make junk. And may the Lord have mercy on the industries that profit from the heresy that he does—the cosmetic and fashion combines that chew up and spit out the self-esteem of men and women. Writing in the eighteenth century, Samuel Johnson said, "Almost every man wastes part of his life in attempts to display qualities which he does not possess, and to gain applause which he cannot keep."[7] I wonder, if he wrote those words today, would he change "part of his life" to "most of his life"? There is great liberty and joy in believing that God don't make no junk, and that all the opinions of all the people in the world do not add up to his opinion of you.

LET YOUR TROUBLES BE TWO-DIMENSIONAL

David finds that being dazzled by God brings peace. In fact, thoughts of God's immensity cure his insomnia. He writes, "How precious to me are your thoughts, O God! / How vast is the sum of them! / Were I to count them, / they would outnumber the grains of sand." Then he adds this odd line: "When I awake, / I am still with you" (Psalm 139:17-18). Here's the picture: David is lying in bed at night counting not sheep but God's thoughts. He's trying to add up all the graces in his life—a cure for the sleeplessness of worry. We too can fall asleep counting the graces from the hand that holds us. We can awake doing the same thing and be at peace. God's thoughts are far greater than the things that trouble us.

Many medieval artists used to paint without using perspective. Their works were two-dimensional, showing only height and breadth. I used to look at these paintings and think, "Didn't they understand depth? Why couldn't they figure out perspective?" Then I learned that many artists painted that way on purpose, out of their conviction as Christians. They believed that if they used perspective in a painting, they were rendering themselves as the ultimate reference point. But only God can stand at the place of ultimate perspective, they reasoned. So as an act of humility and reverence, they left out what they believed only God possessed.

While I disagree with these painters' conclusions as artists, I agree with their premise as Christians. We can let our troubles be two-dimensional. Only God has true perspective on them, and he says, "Do not be anxious about anything, but in everything, by prayer and petition, with thanksgiving, present your requests to God. And the peace of God, which transcends all understanding, will guard your hearts and your minds in Christ Jesus" (Philippians 4:6-7).

George Herbert must have been thinking along these lines when he wrote this poem as a bedtime prayer:

My God, Thou art all love:
Not one poor minute 'scapes Thy breast,
But brings a favor from above;
And in this love, more than in bed I rest.[8]

Love Came and She Didn't Recognize It

When I was in college I had a friend who loved a girl. In some ways they had a marvelous relationship. They could talk about anything; they were best friends; they had tremendous rapport. The only thing wrong was that he didn't look like the man she wanted to marry. She had envisioned a tall, blond, blue-eyed surfer type. But he looked a lot like me. Anything but that!

The disparity between what she'd been looking for and what he looked like became too great and the friendship ended. He shared with me a letter he wrote her. He said goodbye and then closed with these words: "Picture me standing at your back door. I'm five-foot-ten instead of six-foot-four. I weigh 210 instead of 180. My hair is black instead of blond. Look at me one more time and try to believe just for a moment that love came to you looking like that—and you didn't recognize it."

My friend, that is what is at stake here. Love has been coming to us every moment of our lives, reaching for us, holding us in ways we've never realized. Do we recognize him? For the sake of his love and our joy, will we reach for him?

⚜ 7 ⚜

HOW GOOD
AND PLEASANT

No Christian is an only child.

EUGENE PETERSON

How good and pleasant it is / when brothers live together in unity!"
A friend of mine loves to comment on that sentence from Psalm 133 by
saying, "Some things are good but not pleasant, and some things are
pleasant but not good. Only a few things are both good and pleasant."
He is right. I can think of a lot of things that are good but not pleasant,
like root canals and colonoscopies. (This list gets longer as I get older.) I
can also think of many things that are pleasant but not good, like salty
French fries drenched in melted Velveeta with bits of jalapeño peppers
mixed in.

Only a few things merit the unqualified commendation of being good
and pleasant, including what David sings about in Psalm 133: brotherly
unity, people getting along in community. David rhapsodizes about this
kind of harmony, comparing it to some glorious and important symbols
of spiritual health. There is great joy in this unity, he says, "For there the
LORD bestows his blessing, / even life forevermore" (Psalm 133:3).

When I first read this psalm, my thoughts were not nearly so ebul-
lient. Had I written it, I would have said, "It's nice when people get along.
Sure beats the alternative. God probably likes it too. Amen."

A Very Good Deal

In the previous chapter I told the story of how I became a Christian—
how I prayed with the godly, gray-haired Mrs. Dalton after being bribed
with Popsicles. There is a sense in which I can't really improve on the
basic message I believed that day, that the gospel was a very good deal.
But there were nuances and implications to that simple faith that I didn't
understand—and still don't, fully.

The first came in the shock I felt after I told my mother about my decision. At the time, she and my father, though Christians, weren't going
to church and hadn't raised my sister and me in the church. So what did
she do the first Sunday after I invited Jesus to come live in my heart? She
made my sister and me get out of bed and go to church! That was certainly not part of the deal I had made in Good News Club. Had it been,
I would have waited longer to make it. I argued with my mother all the
way to church: "Mrs. Dalton said going to church doesn't make you a
Christian any more than standing in a garage makes you a car. It's a personal relationship with Jesus." Thus began my career in the church—
amid complaint, debate and sophistry.

Søren Kierkegaard said Jesus does two things whenever he sees a
crowd. The first is to disburse it and isolate each individual with himself.
The second is to take those he has separated out and reintroduce them
to each other. He dismisses the crowd to transform it into a community
he calls the church and the Bible shockingly calls his family, even his
body. He wants a personal relationship with every human being, and he
wants them to be personally involved with each other.

"We can no more be a Christian and have nothing to do with the
church than we can be a person and not be in a family," writes Eugene
Peterson. "For God never makes private, secret salvation deals with people. His relationships with us are personal, true; intimate, yes; but private, no. We are a family in Christ. When we become Christians, we are
among brothers and sisters in faith. No Christian is an only child."[1]

He Brings His Whole Family In with Him

So Mrs. Dalton was mostly right. Jesus indeed stands at the door of each heart and knocks. But the verse she quoted, Revelation 3:20, was written to a church, a community. Jesus wants to be in each of his people and among them all. What I didn't understand at the moment of my conversion was that inviting Jesus into my heart meant he would bring his whole family in with him!

What Peter Taylor Forsyth said about prayer applies equally to the significance of the church:

> Our egoism retires before the coming of God, and into the clearance there comes with our Father, our brother. We realize man as he is in God and for God, his Lover. When God fills our heart he makes more room for man than the humanist heart can find. Prayer is an act, indeed the act of fellowship.[2]

In fact, all Christian prayer is in the church, for Jesus said to pray to God as "our Father" (Matthew 6:9).

I still have a lot to learn about the Christian life. What I'm learning now is that it's not only about Jesus and me, it's about Jesus and us, and the good and pleasant joy David sang of in Psalm 133. Remember, joy is what we feel when we are grateful for the grace given us. In this case the grace is the church. To receive this gift with proper gratitude is to know the deep gladness of unity in Christ.

The best place in the Gospels to witness Christ's passion for the church is in the prayer he prayed before his arrest and crucifixion. It was the last thing he did before they took him away. He prayed that his people "may be one, Father, just as . . . we are one: I in them and you in me. May they be brought to complete unity" (John 17:21-23). The wildest dreams of human utopia cannot touch this. Jesus actually prayed that the good and pleasant fellowship of his church would be like the eternal fellowship of the Godhead: Father, Son and Holy Spirit. For God himself is a community. According to Jesus' prayer, then, the church is to be quite literally a little bit of heaven on earth. This is a key part of the mystery that states we may "participate in the divine nature and escape the corruption in the world" (2 Peter 1:4).

Jesus linked love for God with love for others. He said the first and greatest commandment is to love God with our whole being. The second is like it: that we love our neighbor as we love ourselves (Matthew 22:34-40). What is so breathtaking about his prayer for the church is that love for each other is not only a corollary to love for God but also the arena in which we experience the love of God.

THE FIRST TIME I KNEW GOD LOVED ME

I remember the very moment I knew, for the first time in my life, that God loved me. It was in November 1963 as I walked across the commons to my dorm room at what was then La Verne College. I even remember what I was wearing—jeans and a white T-shirt. As I walked, it was as though Christ came along beside me like he did with the disciples on the road to Emmaus. He seemed to smile and speak personally of his deep affection for me.

I had been a Christian for years at that point. I knew God loved me in a general sort of way: I had wept many times when I thought of what he did for me on the cross. But somehow it had seemed like his love for me was a great altruistic operation undertaken with a long-suffering sigh. I never felt he actually took any delight in me as a person; rather, his love was so great it could overcome even his disgust at my bad habits. But now I could sense without a doubt that he loved me—and even liked me.

I wondered, why now? What had happened? As I reflected on recent events in my life, I knew the answer: I had been experiencing good and pleasant Christian community in the past three months. My closest friends consisted of a fine group of Christian men. As students will do, we often found ourselves talking into the wee hours of the morning. As the hour grew late and we got tired, something personal would sometimes slip into our conversation. Perhaps I would accidentally reveal that I had thought or done something I was sure no one else had ever thought or done. There would be an agonizing moment of silence when I wondered if they would all get up and leave the room in disgust, or laugh at me. Then one of my friends would say, "You too? I thought I was the only one."

In those three months the real me, Ben Patterson as he was inside and outside, was becoming known and loved. It was a little bit of heaven. As small as it was, that realization was joyful and life-changing, and it was a signpost to the profound reality Jesus prayed for the night he was betrayed.

THE CENTRIFUGAL POWER OF SIN

But Jesus was praying for something even bigger: the kind of community only God can create. My college buddies and I had a lot in common, and in some ways the intimacy we knew wasn't that surprising. It can be approximated in purely secular settings by people willing to risk a little self-disclosure. Don't get me wrong—what we experienced together was godly and genuinely spiritual, something included in Jesus' prayer in John 17. But Christ was praying for unity not only among the most likely people. His was a prayer to break down seemingly insurmountable walls of race, gender and ethnicity, between male and female, slave and free, Jew and Gentile, and to make them one in the good and pleasant fellowship of his church. His purpose in going to the cross was "to reconcile to himself all things, whether things on earth or things in heaven, by making peace through his blood, shed on the cross" (Colossians 1:20).

Clearly, only God can create this kind of community by the power of his Holy Spirit. That is the message of Pentecost, when people from all over the world, thronging the streets of Jerusalem, heard the gospel preached in their native tongues (Acts 2:1-12). The Spirit was blowing through the church, birthing fellowship. As he did, he reversed the damage of Babel, when humankind in its pride decided to build a tower reaching to the heavens. Their goal? To "make a name for ourselves and not be scattered over the face of the whole earth" (Genesis 11:4).

The irony of all sin is its unintended consequences. The very thing the people sought to avoid with their grand ego-structure was the very thing that happened. God confused their language, turning one into many, and they lost their ability to communicate. What unity they had was lost, and they were scattered over the face of the earth. That's what sin does to community. Its power is centrifugal. Frederick Buechner writes, "When at work in a human life, [sin] tends to push everything out toward the periphery. Bits and pieces go flying off until only the core is left.

Eventually bits and pieces of the core itself go flying off until in the end nothing at all is left."[3]

"Let's make a name for ourselves!" That is the demonic side of multiculturalism—and it's been around from the beginning. On the other hand, a community in which individuality and diversity thrive and feed the whole, and are in turn fed by the whole, is beautiful. It's also extremely rare—miraculous, really. But that is the miracle of Pentecost: it is the answer to Jesus' prayer in John 17, the joy of Christian community.

MR. BROWN SUIT MEETS MR. FLIP-FLOPS

In my years as a pastor I saw some wonderful and hilarious Pentecostal miracles. One involved a young man I'll call Dave. The first time I saw Dave he was standing in the back of the sanctuary as I preached, arms folded skeptically over his chest, wearing a wetsuit. His hair was matted and wet from surfing earlier that morning. His appearance would have been remarkable in almost any church, but to fully appreciate how he stood out, you need to know the kind of congregation I was pastoring at the time. It was in Irvine, California, an upscale community in south Orange County. Our parking lot was full of BMWs, Mercedes and the requisite minivans of a church of young families. Most of our members were professionals, and though they were casual Southern Californians, their attire was on the nice end of casual. Dave clearly did not come from Irvine.

When we met I learned he had never been in a church before that day, and he had grown up virtually on the streets in a nearby beach town. His van in the parking lot said it all: it was plastered with bumper stickers advertising Dos Equis and Corona. Its interior was green shag carpet, with surfboards stacked on one side and crushed cans (also advertising his refreshment of choice) scattered about. In numerous ways Dave was unique—and a total anomaly in our good and pleasant little Christian community.

But God wanted to make us better and more pleasant. In the months that followed, Dave was embraced by the church and soon became a Christian. He was with us for years and I can't recall him ever being dressed in anything more formal than sandals, gym shorts and a T-shirt that often advertised a beer, a raceway or a surfboard manufacturer. But now he was carrying a Bible. I loved this guy.

One year the church hosted a pastors' conference. It was a two-day event, requiring that our congregation provide beds and breakfast for the sixty pastors who would attend. I asked my people to sign up, and soon every pastor had a host family. At the end of the first day of the conference, cars began arriving to pick up their guests for the night. Soon every pastor was gone except one. He was a little man from a farming town in the central valley of California. He wore thick glasses and a conservative brown suit with a thin dark tie, and he carried a large Bible. Everything about him said rectitude, provinciality, control. He stood smiling and waiting patiently for his host to appear.

I checked the list to see who he had been matched with. It was Dave! Surfer Dave! Dos Equis Dave! I gasped in alarm. This was not a good match, not a good match at all. For a moment I considered calling Dave to tell him we didn't need his help after all and checking this man into a local motel. I may have done just that if Dave had not at that moment careened into the parking lot, tires squealing. So I had no choice but to introduce them to each other. Dave swung open the side door of his van. The passenger seat was out because Dave had been working on the engine, which was accessible only from the inside of the vehicle. So the pastor had to sit on the green shag carpet amid the crushed beer cans and surfboards. I laughed nervously as I helped him with his luggage. As they drove off I resigned myself to being the pastor who was responsible for giving these two men the worst night of their lives.

The next morning the host families began to drop off the pastors at the church. One by one they arrived until all were present except—you guessed it—Dave and the conservative little pastor. Just before the first meeting was to start, I saw Dave's van come roaring into the parking lot. Through the glare of the windshield I could see the faces of Dave and the pastor—and they were laughing! Uproariously. As they got out of the van they exchanged addresses, Mr. Brown Suit and Mr. Flip-Flops. They were like two kids who had become best friends at summer camp. Each told me he had had the time of his life.

I remember feeling three things that morning as I walked into the meeting. One was embarrassment at my fear the night before. I had sold both men short. The second was wonder at the power of the Holy Spirit to create a near-miraculous bond of love between the least likely people. I had sold God short too. The third was a renewed joy in the good and pleasant fellowship of the church. All three were little answers to the prayer Jesus prayed in John 17.

A PERSUASIVE UNITY

We live in a divided world. Deep hatred separates Croats and Serbs, Hutus and Tutsis, Jews and Arabs, men and women, rich and poor. Only the supernatural unity of the Holy Spirit can bring these people together. Whenever it happens, the world takes notice because it's so rare. The impact is so great that Jesus ascribed to this kind of unity a supernatural power produced by nothing else: the power to persuade the world that he is who he says he is. He prayed, "May they be brought to complete unity to let the world know that you sent me" (John 17:23). According to Jesus, the greatest argument for the reality of the incarnation, God-become-man, does not come from philosophers and theologians. The greatest apologetic for the faith comes from Christians who live in the unity of the Holy Spirit.

The tendency of modern American culture toward isolated individualism is death to the church's witness of the reality of Jesus. Archbishop William Temple panned this inclination when he wrote, tongue-in-cheek, "I believe in one holy, infallible church, of which I regret to say that at the present time I am the only member." So much for the power of many voices speaking as one—instead one voice speaks as many. Economist R. H. Tawney was thinking along the same lines when he declared that the man who "seeks God apart from his brethren is likely not to find God, but rather the devil, whose face will bear a surprising resemblance to his own."[4]

It's obvious why individualistic attitudes vitiate the witness of the church. When Peter gave his ringing confession of faith in Christ, Jesus' response was to announce that Peter would build his church and that hell itself would not stand against it (Matthew 16:16-19). But clearly, if the members of the church refuse to be built, if the living stones will not be fit together (Ephesians 2:19-22; 1 Peter 2:5-6), then the church will fall far short of its purpose as the powerful presence of Christ's kingdom in the world.

Unity has this kind of power because when we live together in love and harmony it can mean only one thing: that we have ceased being our own little lords and submitted to the one Lord. When Christ is truly Lord over his people, his power is released into the world. The lordship of Jesus Christ is meant to start in the church and radiate outward, drawing people to himself.

One of the most important ways we show our submission to the Lord Christ is by yielding to each other for his sake. "Submit to one another out of reverence for Christ," writes Paul (Ephesians 5:21). The genius of this command is that it makes love practical and real. It's easy to say we love Jesus as long as there is no flesh-and-blood Jesus to deal with. The "spiritual" love we claim to feel for him in our thoughts and emotions often stays there: in our thoughts and emotions. The only way to show we really love Jesus is to love his flesh-and-blood people. Anything less is sentimentality and self-deception. John the apostle puts it bluntly: "For anyone who does not love his brother, whom he has seen, cannot love God, whom he has not seen" (1 John 4:20). You cannot love Jesus and in any way despise his people.

NIGHT OF FIRE

I don't think I ever seriously thought about these truths until I read Blaise Pascal's account of his transforming encounter with God. It is one of the loveliest descriptions of the joy of God's presence in all of literature. To read it is to ache with longing for the same experience. He described the encounter with one word: "fire." It produced in him:

Certainty, certainty, heartfelt, joy, peace.
God of Jesus Christ.
God of Jesus Christ. . . .
Joy, joy, joy, tears of joy.[5]

And it brought to him certain convictions, such as:

> He can only be found by the ways taught in the Gospels. . . .
> "And this is life eternal, that they might know thee, the only true
> God, and Jesus Christ whom thou hast sent."
> Jesus Christ.
> Jesus Christ. . . .
> He can only be kept by the ways taught in the Gospel.
> Sweet and total renunciation.
> Total submission to Jesus Christ and my director.
> Everlasting joy in return for one day's effort on earth.
> I will not forget thy word. Amen.[6]

This is all very appealing to modern religious sensibilities, in which private experience and ecstasy are highly sought. Everyone wants "joy, joy, joy, tears of joy." But look more closely. Though Pascal's experience was intensely personal, it was not private. For Pascal, overwhelming joy and certainty led him straight to something that sounds a little strange to us: "Total submission to Jesus Christ and my director." The "Jesus Christ" part makes sense. But who is this director? And submission to him—what's that about?

Pascal, a Roman Catholic, was associated with a renewal movement called Jansenism. The spiritual guidelines of the Jansenist community required that each member be in practical submission to a spiritual director, one who guided their Christian walk. They knew submission to Jesus would be no more than theoretical if it didn't translate into a concrete relationship with a flesh-and-blood member of Christ's church. If submission wasn't practical, it wasn't real. It certainly must have been practical for Pascal. Here he was, one of the greatest minds Western civilization had ever seen, humbly placing himself under a man who was most likely his intellectual inferior. But that didn't matter. Brains, beauty and power are beside the point. Pascal believed that before the Infinite, all finites are the same. He was submitting for the sake of Christ.

The church, the body of Christ, is no mere mental construct; it is real. Loyalty to Christ means loyalty to his church or it is not really loyalty to

Christ. To say we love Jesus but not his church is a false dichotomy. The two are inseparable. "Conversion means conversion to the Church, to the Body of Christ," writes Peter Kreeft. "The Church is not an addition after conversion; the Church is an aspect of conversion. Romeo doesn't marry Juliet's body after he marries Juliet!"[7] As Pascal understood in that night of fire, not only can Jesus be found only by the ways taught in the Gospels; he can only be kept by the ways taught in the Gospels. Do we love Jesus? Then we must love his body.

PRECIOUS TO EACH OTHER

Jesus prayed that we would be one even as he and his Father are one. This good and pleasant unity demonstrates to the world the reality of Jesus; it also shows them that we are a blessed people. "I in them and you in me," he prayed. "May they be brought to complete unity to let the world know that you sent me and have loved them even as you have loved me" (John 17:23). Unity shows the world that God loves us. When we are precious to each other, we demonstrate that we are precious to God.

Loving each other can be hard work, but it can be great fun once we get past some of the initial discomfort. Mr. Brown Suit and Mr. Flip-Flops would agree. Sometimes we have to grit our teeth and love a brother before we can like him. Sometimes we must pray for the strength to will a sister's good long before we find her good or pleasant. But the rewards will come—if we "do not become weary in doing good, for at the proper time we will reap a harvest" (Galatians 6:9).

The harvest is the fruit of the Spirit, of which love and joy are first (Galatians 5:22-23). Fruit is an apt metaphor, for joy in the church is like farming: it involves plowing and planting and watering and feeding and waiting. Especially waiting. Ninety percent of life in the church is just showing up, again and again, until the harvest comes. "Let us not give up meeting together, as some are in the habit of doing, but let us encourage one another" (Hebrews 10:25). Wonderful things happen when we do.

A graduate student in anthropology spent a summer doing research in a Navajo village. He lived with one of the families as he did his work, and as the weeks passed he was treated like a family member. He grew especially close to the mother. When it came time to leave, the village gave him a going-away party. Throughout the festivities, the student noticed that the mother was unusually quiet and subdued. After it was over, when everyone had gone home, he sat down beside her to talk awhile before going to bed and back to the university the next morning. He asked if she was all right. She struggled to answer in her broken English. The words came slowly: "I . . . like me . . . best . . . when I am . . . with . . . you."

Because that is what Jesus prays for us, that is the way it can be in the church. It is radically transforming and deeply joyful to live in a community where I am free to become the best possible me, and you are free to become the best possible you. How persuasive of the gospel! How good and pleasant it is!

8

WORDS THAT GIVE LIFE

Kind words are the music of the world.
They have a power that seems to be beyond natural causes,
as if they were some angel's song that had lost its way and come on earth.
It seems as if they could almost do what in reality only God can do—
soften the hard and angry hearts of men.
No one was ever corrected by a sarcasm—
crushed, perhaps, if the sarcasm was clever enough,
but drawn nearer to God, never.

FREDERICK FABER

In the summer of 1954, before my seventh grade year, my parents did a terrible thing to me: they moved—three times. We moved to a new neighborhood in June, another in July and finally, two weeks into the school year, yet another. I spent the entire summer between sixth and seventh grade in communities where I knew nobody. What made this so awful was that the school districts we drifted through were infamous for the hazing of little seventh grade boys by big eighth and ninth graders in the first week of school. Horror stories circulated all summer about boys like me having lipstick smeared all over their faces, having Vaseline massaged into their hair, or the worst, being "pantsed"—having their pants forcibly removed and being left to languish in their underwear in front of a laughing crowd.

I was desperate that summer to make at least one friend who was a big guy, an eighth or ninth grader who might defend me that first week of school, or at least mitigate the torture of his peers. Throughout July and August, the only candidates in sight were two ninth graders who lived down the street and who hung out together every day. But they paid me no mind. Actually, it was worse than that: they appeared to deliberately pay me no mind, which means they were in fact paying a lot of attention—with malicious intent.

Something had to be done. But what? One morning as I sat at the picnic table in my backyard, the idea came to me. I had just finished building a model airplane and was examining the many partially used bottles of paint I had used on other projects. Building model airplanes had been my solitary pursuit that summer. My eyes moved back and forth between the paint and my worn-out, black, high-top sneakers—U.S. Keds Flyers, as I recall. Paint and shoes, shoes and paint; bingo! I would use the leftover paint to decorate my sneakers with flames and lightning bolts!

I began immediately. Remember, it was the summer of 1954; this kind of thing wouldn't become popular until the late '60s. I was way ahead of my time. When the paint dried, I sat and admired my craftsmanship. Now was the time to make my move on the two big guys down the street. When they saw the bold and imaginative pieces of art I had created out of my shoes, they would realize at long last that I was a person worthy of at least their protection, if not their friendship and admiration.

I put the shoes on and walked down the street. The boys were together as usual, and obviously saw me coming as they sat on the front porch. But like always they acted as though they didn't. Undeterred, I lifted my feet a little higher. Perhaps they hadn't seen the shoes yet. I practically goose-stepped up to them, stood there for a moment with a cocky grin, and said, "Hi guys." They stared at me. It could only have been for a few seconds, but I felt as though I had aged forty years when one of them finally spoke and said, "Those shoes are the stupidest things I have ever seen." My field of vision narrowed; I think I almost blacked out. I mumbled something I can't remember and walked back home, with low steps this time, and threw my stupid multicolored sneakers into the trash.

My first week of seventh grade was miserable.

It's a Lie

You know the saying, "Sticks and stones may break my bones, but words will never hurt me"? Like me, you probably had a point in your life when you realized it was a lie. Bones broken by sticks and stones usually mend. But wounds inflicted by words may never heal. Even now as I tell that story, more than forty years later, I feel my cheeks flush with a tinge of embarrassment and shame. But it works the other way too. Our words have an awesome power to do good, to impart grace and therefore to bring joy. In fact, our use of words can be a discipline of joy.

The power of human words is grounded in the power of God's word. When God speaks, he doesn't just utter sounds and signs and symbols; he speaks deeds and actions. He creates with words. In the Genesis account of creation, he says, "Let there be light," and there is light. He isn't wrestling with preexistent material; he's not trying to carve something out of a primeval glob. He just says it and it is.

Later on in the Bible we are told that whenever God wants to do something, he simply sends forth his word from his mouth, and it is as if he himself goes down and does it. He says, "As the rain and the snow / come down from heaven, / and do not return to it / without watering the earth / and making it bud and flourish, / so that it yields seed for the sower and bread for the eater, / so is my word that goes out from my mouth: / It will not return to me empty, / but will accomplish what I desire / and achieve the purpose for which I sent it" (Isaiah 55:10-11).

The gospel makes it clear that when God sends out his word, it is God himself who goes. His word is Jesus Christ, God incarnate, the second person of the Holy Trinity: "In the beginning was the Word, and the Word was with God, and the Word was God. . . . Through him all things were made; without him nothing was made that has been made. . . . The Word became flesh and made his dwelling among us. We have seen his glory, the glory of the One and Only, who came from the Father, full of grace and truth" (John 1:1, 3, 14). When God spoke his heart to us, he spoke Jesus, full of grace and truth. He used the almighty power of his word to bless, not to curse; to create, not to destroy.

Since we are made in God's image, it should not surprise us that our words also have power. They are more than signs and symbols; they are deeds and actions. Something of us goes out when we speak and accomplishes the purpose we intended. The ancient Hebrews understood this better than we do. When Jacob duped his father Isaac into giving him the blessing intended for his brother Esau (Genesis 27), Isaac could not take back the words he had spoken. They had gone out and done their work.

Modern Westerners read this story and are puzzled. We wonder, why couldn't Isaac just revoke the blessing and give it to the one he meant it for? We think that way because we regard words lightly. We have reduced them to mere sounds and designations. But I think in our hearts we know better. Has anyone ever lashed out at you in anger, later regretted it and apologized by saying something like, "I didn't mean it"? You may have accepted the apology, but the words were agents of the person who spoke them, and they did their work. You may forgive and be healed, but you know the words were meant when they were spoken, and you know the damage they did.

THE INCARNATION IN MINIATURE

Jesus' view is that we mean what we say, because what we say reveals who we are inside. He said, "For out of the overflow of the heart the mouth speaks. The good man brings good things out of the good stored up in him, and the evil man brings evil things out of the evil stored up in him. But I tell you that men will have to give account on the day of judgment for every careless word they have spoken. For by your words you will be acquitted, and by your words you will be condemned" (Matthew 12:34-37).

God wants us to speak our words to others in the same gracious way he spoke his word to us in Jesus Christ. He wants our speech to be the incarnation in miniature, full of grace and truth. "Let your conversation be always full of grace, seasoned with salt" (Colossians 4:6). Salt was a preservative and flavor enhancer in ancient times—and it still is. Kindness, affirmation and gentleness of speech hold families and communities together. Much more, they make them joyous places to be. In a culture of gracious speech, where our words to each other are like the word God spoke to us in Christ, people flourish and grow and become themselves. Families and churches become places where God is glorified and people are made glad.

That's why the apostle Paul so often says things like, "Let the word of Christ dwell in you richly as you teach and admonish one another with all wisdom, and as you sing psalms, hymns and spiritual songs with gratitude in your hearts to God" (Colossians 3:16). In fact, the apostle says to shun all words that curse and speak only words that impart grace and truth. "Do not let any unwholesome talk come out of your mouths, but only what is helpful for building others up according to their needs, that it may benefit those who listen" (Ephesians 4:29). He sets up two opposing and mutually exclusive categories. There is to be no unwholesome talk, and there is to be only helpful talk. Period. No qualifications.

Paul's Greek vocabulary is revealing. The word translated "unwholesome" is *sapros,* a word used of rotten fruit and a good picture of the way negative speech affects a community. One piece of decaying fruit in a bowl will inevitably spoil the rest. Every insult, every juicy tidbit of gossip, every coarse joke is an invitation for others to join in. In fact, they are more than invitations; they are nudges and even friendly shoves. And there are many other ways we can bully others into dismantling a person's reputation and self-esteem. Sometimes words aren't even necessary. An arched eyebrow or a pregnant silence can do the same damage. In C. S. Lewis's *The Screwtape Letters,* the devil Screwtape advises his nephew Wormwood on the powerful nuances of these temptations to rottenness when he speaks of the "subtle play of looks and tones and laughs by which a mortal can imply that he is of the same party as those to whom he is speaking." All we need do is be silent when we ought to speak and laugh when we ought to be silent.[1] Without overtly committing ourselves, we can be *sapros.*

A THREEFOLD POISON

Paul uses other words to broaden his picture of *sapros*. All delineate the nuances of rotten speech. "Get rid of all bitterness, rage and anger, brawling and slander, along with every form of malice" (Ephesians 4:31). A good way to think of "brawling" is as public rottenness and "slander" as a more private variety. The word translated "brawling" is used in the Greek to describe public outcry. It can be an insult shouted across a room or a savage letter to the editor. It is meanness, derision and harshness taken to the streets. The word translated "slander" connotes a more quiet version of the same thing: something said behind a person's back, perhaps in private.

"Rage" is a hair-trigger temper. "Anger" is a more settled, habitual, smoldering wrath. Rage explodes; anger oozes. "Malice" is general ill will and bad feeling toward others. "Bitterness" is longstanding, brooding resentment and rancor. Over time, it shrivels the soul as nothing else can—like the old man who was asked if he ever intended to end a thirty-year feud that had kept him and a brother apart. "Nope," he replied. "I can't. The bastard up and died on me." Brawling and slander, rage and anger are the things we do. Bitterness and malice are why we do them. The former are the fruit, the latter are the root. All are rotten.

Who is hurt by these things? Everyone! Charles Spurgeon called *sapros* speech a threefold poison. First, the person spoken against is poisoned. Living in this fallen world means feeling the toxins of words spoken against us coursing through our souls. When I was young and more naive, I was frankly a little skeptical of the Bible's harsh assessment of *sapros* speech—were people's mouths really like open graves, their words like viper's poison, their tongues like sharp swords and arrows? It seemed a bit exaggerated. But I have since experienced the lonely pain of walking into a room that grew quieter when I entered. I have come to know firsthand how hopeless it is to set right what was made wrong by lying and slander. The bigger and more outrageous the lie, and the harder someone tries to set the record straight, the more suspicious the truth telling seems. People's eyes assert, along with Shakespeare, "The lady [or the man] doth protest too much." Undoing the damage of *sapros* speech is like cutting away the heads of Hydra; for each head severed, two more grow back. The damage is as enduring as it is incalculable.

Second, the person who speaks is also poisoned. Have you ever felt dirty after you've engaged in *sapros* speech? I have. There's a good reason for this effect, and Jesus explains it. He says I'm tasting the offal of my rotten soul on my lips. Many religious teachers of his day thought people were polluted by what they ate, by what went into them. Jesus said it was the other way around: people are polluted by what comes out of them. "Don't you see that whatever enters the mouth goes into the stomach and then out of the body? But the things that come out of the mouth come from the heart, and these make a man 'unclean.' For out of the heart come evil thoughts, murder, adultery, sexual immorality, theft, false testimony, slander. These are what make a man 'unclean'" (Matthew 15:17-20). In other words, it's not what goes in that's dirty; it's what comes out. When we sin with our tongues, that's what we taste on our tongues: soul dung.

Third, in a less obvious but much more important way, the Holy Spirit of God is hurt. In reference to *sapros* speech, Paul says, "And do not grieve the Holy Spirit of God, with whom you were sealed for the day of redemption" (Ephesians 4:30). It is unfathomable to me that our silly little word battles can hurt God. But they can. Certainly it must have something to do with his great love for us—people who were made in his image and bought with the blood of his Son. When those he loves are damaged by unwholesome words, he grieves, whether they are perpetrators or victims.

THROUGH THE FATHER'S EYES

When I was in fifth grade I developed a strong dislike for a boy I'll call Dennis. I think the reason for my antipathy had something to do with the fact that he wore his shirts buttoned all the way to the top. You need to understand that in Compton, California, at Abraham Lincoln Elementary School in 1950, it was most uncool of boys to wear their shirts with the top button buttoned. So naturally I felt I had to punish him for this breach of custom and manliness. As I write this, I am appalled at how natural it seemed to me then to act so foolishly and hurtfully. One day at lunch I challenged him to a fight after school the next day. To help the lesson sink in, I wanted him to worry for twenty-four hours about what was going to happen.

The next morning as I was walking to school, I saw Dennis a few blocks away getting out of his father's car. His dad had driven him to school and was getting out of the car to give his son a hug and kiss before he left. I watched as his dad knelt down to Dennis's level and drew the boy into his big arms. I saw Dennis wrap his little arms around his dad's neck. They were talking quietly, and from where I stood I could see Dennis smile at something his dad said. Then I watched his dad kiss him on the cheek, run his hand playfully over the boy's head, get back in the car and drive away. The whole scene lasted only a few seconds, but it was like slow motion to my consciousness. Time slowed down and I was forced, against my will, to see Dennis through his dad's eyes. I couldn't fight him that afternoon. Everything had changed. He was no longer just Dennis-with-his-shirt-buttoned-at-the-neck. He was now Dennis, his dad's son, precious and beloved.

The same truth underlies the Bible's condemnation of violence of any kind, verbal or physical. Every victim of violence is a person made in the image of God, cherished and beloved, someone for whom Christ shed his blood and died (see Genesis 9:6; Acts 20:28; James 3:9). Every perpetrator of violence is also a precious creation. And when humans engage in cruelty and destructiveness toward each other, God takes it personally. Once David fully realized the enormity of what he had done in committing adultery with Bathsheba and arranging for the murder of her husband, Uriah, he said to God, "Against you, you only, have I sinned / and done what is evil in your sight" (Psalm 51:4). His sin included Bathsheba and Uriah, but ultimately it was committed against the God who made them in his image. Their worth was grounded in the infinite worth of their Creator. Naturally God is grieved when *sapros* talk of any kind affects those he loves.

But the most profound reason God grieves at violence is that he himself is a community of Father, Son and Holy Spirit. He lives in an eternal fellowship of love. People who hurt and destroy one another with words are acting in direct opposition to who God is in himself and what he wants for us in Christ. They are, in fact, working against the very thing for which Jesus prayed on the night he was arrested: "I in them and you in me. May they be brought to complete unity to let the world know that you sent me and have loved them even as you have loved me" (John 17:23). So very much is riding on the words we speak! Our unity will actually convince the world of the truth of the gospel message. Disunity, of course, will do just the opposite. And it will block our entry into the supreme joy of the fellowship of the Godhead—a fellowship Jesus died to bring us into.

I speak of a glory and a mystery that is beyond my rational capabilities. But one thing is clear: Christ so passionately desires this community of love that it was among the last things he asked his Father for on the night he died (see also John 13:34-35). It was his passion and his mission. Joni Eareckson Tada said it well: "Words. Do you fully understand their power? Can any of us really grasp the mighty force behind the things we say? Do we stop and think before we speak, considering the potency of the phrases we utter?"[2]

INTERDICT AND INTERRUPT IT

Other than refusing to speak *sapros* ourselves, the best thing we can do is refuse to listen to it. It thrives on listening ears, especially among friends. We say, "Friends don't let friends drive drunk." Why not say, "Friends don't listen to friends who speak *sapros*"? John Wesley and his friends thought this was a good idea. In 1752 they signed a covenant, which hung on the wall of each individual's home. The agreement amounted to a six-point defense against *sapros* speech. The eighteenth-century language is a little cumbersome to modern ears, so I'll add some of my own commentary in italics.

- That we will not listen or willingly inquire after ill concerning one another. (*We won't listen to it and we won't look for it.*)

- That, if we do hear any ill of each other, we will not be forward to believe it. (*Everyone will be considered innocent until proven guilty.*)

- That as soon as possible we will communicate what we hear by speaking or writing to the person concerned. (*Do you want to shut down* sapros *talk real quick? Tell the person speaking it that you intend to inform the person being spoken against.*)

- That until we have done this, we will not write or speak a syllable of it to any other person. (*No more talk until this is done.*)

- That neither will we mention it, after we have done this, to any other person. (*No more talk after this is done.*)

- That we will not make exception to any of these rules unless we think ourselves absolutely obliged in conference. (*We will make no exceptions to any of the above unless, after conferring with one another, we believe ourselves compelled to do so.*)

To interdict and interrupt *sapros* speech is an effective though somewhat negative approach to the problem. A better tactic is to practice the opposite: speak only words that impart grace and truth. Paul recommended this to the Ephesians, urging them to speak "only what is helpful for building others up according to their needs, that it may benefit those who listen" (4:29). Gracious speech has three characteristics: it is constructive (building others up), it is tailor-made for those who hear it (according to their needs), and it imparts grace (benefits those who listen). The word translated "benefit" in this text is stronger in the Greek. It literally means "impart grace." Before we speak, we should ask ourselves, Will what I say build up and impart grace to those who hear? Will my words contain something of the gospel? Will they, like the grace of the Lord Jesus Christ, evoke a response of gratitude and joy?

CALL FORTH THE BEST

Gracious words build up and strengthen others, calling forth their best. I read of a professor at a small New England college who year after year was voted by his colleagues and students as the school's outstanding instructor. When he retired, the college held a banquet in his honor and asked him to give a speech explaining the secret to his success as a teacher. The professor blushed as he began and said, "Well, I guess I can say it now that I'm leaving. At the beginning of every semester, in every class I taught, I would identify the student who seemed most likely to fail. On the first exam, I gave this person a far better grade than he or she deserved. And then I somehow made it known to the rest of the class, in the student's hearing, how well the student had done. In forty years of teaching, it never failed to produce the desired result. Every student rose to a higher level."

Any hack can tear down; it takes a real artist to build up. You will never see a monument in a city erected to a critic. When Jacques Plante, the great National Hockey League goalie, retired, someone asked him how he had liked being a goalie. He quipped, "How would you like a job where if you make a mistake, a big red light goes on and eighteen thousand people boo?" Families can be like that. Churches and institutions and whole communities can be that way too. And they pass on with inexorable regularity these traits from generation to generation.

RITES OF AFFIRMATION

How much better for families and communities to be cultures of "building others up according to their needs" and imparting grace "to those who listen." I am blessed with a wife who is a great builder-upper, and we've tried to raise our children to be this way. We have a family birthday tradition I really love—a kind of "rite of affirmation." Churches have their sacraments and symbols that point to profound realities; the Pattersons have their birthday tradition. The way it works is simple: we bombard the birthday person with compliments. If it's my birthday I hear from all my family members, and whoever else is present, everything they admire and love about me!

I won't tell you what they say about me, but if it's my daughter, Mary, being celebrated, I tell her I love the way she laughs so hard that tears squirt out her eyes like little saline projectiles. I let her know what a thoughtful and interesting person she is, how I love her kindness and what a pleasure it is to take a walk with her. Her mother and brothers and friends also speak their appreciation. She grows quiet and warm and even more beautiful. And her eyes show how hungrily her heart drinks it in. She is enlarged in her soul, made deeper and stronger. Although she and her brothers are now young adults, they still respond the same way. So does my wife. So do I. So would you, I believe. This kind of grace evokes joyful gratitude in all who hear.

Throughout my life, the people who most influenced me for the good were without exception the people who related to me this way. When I was in college and seminary I had a boss who treated me with affirmation and grace over and over again. His name was Jim Slevcove, and to this day I count him among my dearest friends. For six summers he was my supervisor at a Christian conference center in California called Forest Home. I'll tell one story that represents this man's ways with me.

Most of the trouble I got into during those summers was related to youthful exuberance: I just couldn't pass up an opportunity to play a prank or engage in a little playful mayhem. But since I held a position of fairly serious responsibility over junior high and high school kids, some of my fun spilled over into crass irresponsibility—like the time I passed off a laxative gum as chewing gum to some of my coworkers. It was part of a friendly rivalry that had been going on for some time, but the results were far worse than I had planned on.

When word got back to Jim, he called and asked me to come to his office for "a little chat." The appointment was for the next day at 4:30. At first I was confident and defiant, with a powerful arsenal of arguments ready for my defense. But I had to wait twenty-four hours before I could unleash my sophistry, and I was worried about what Jim was going to do. When I arrived at his office the next day, the arguments didn't seem so compelling, and I fidgeted as I waited, trying to think of some new ones. He finally called me in at five o'clock, well past the appointed time. I sat down and he sat down. There was a long, awkward silence as he leaned back in his chair and looked up at the ceiling. I was still a little defiant but no longer confident.

I watched his eyes for the slightest flicker of what was coming. Wait; were those tears in his eyes or the effects of a summer allergy? They were tears! Then he spoke. "Benny," he whispered softly. That's all, just "Benny." No one called me Benny anymore. I was Ben, a young adult, a man. Benny sounded like a little boy, or worse, a character in a Damon Runyon musical, Benny the Bookie. Benny wasn't smart enough to have powerful arguments. But the way he said it was full of tender affection, and I almost burst into tears when he said it again. And again—just "Benny." That's all he said until he got control of his emotions.

The next words he spoke I don't remember. But they didn't matter. My arguments disappeared like the vapor they were. I was wrong. I had gone way over the line of propriety, not to mention compassion—the laxative proved to be a rigorous purgative. I owed and paid him and my victims an apology. And more important, Jim and I had a good conversation about the issues in my life this episode touched on: my impulsiveness and vindictiveness, the meaning of Christian community and the responsibilities that go with leadership. This was always his pattern. Even in saying the hard thing to me he was gracious. His goal was not to tear down but to build up. And if a little tearing down was necessary, it was always for the sake of building up. He said no in order to say a bigger yes. Rebuke, when it came, was often accompanied by tears. He was always looking for a way to say I love you, building me up according to my needs, imparting grace that called forth thankfulness, joy and my very best as a young man.

Each of us can do the same for others. Our words can be like the kiss a young man gave his wife after surgery. Dr. Richard Selzer recalls the scene. He has just performed a mostly successful surgery on a woman's face; the malignant tumor in her cheek is gone, but in order to remove it he's had to cut a little nerve to her mouth. Her mouth is now twisted and palsied, almost clownish, and will be for the rest of her life. The cancer is gone, but so is the beautiful mouth she once had. Selzer watches as her husband

> stands on the opposite side of the bed, and together they seem to dwell in the evening lamplight, isolated from me, private. Who are they, I ask myself, he and this wry-mouth I have made, who gaze at and touch each other so generously, greedily? The young woman speaks. "Will my mouth always be like this?" she asks.

"Yes," I say, "it will. It is because the nerve was cut." She nods and is silent. But the young man smiles. "I like it," he says. "It is kind of cute." All at once I *know* who he is. I understand, and I lower my gaze. One is not bold in an encounter with a god. Unmindful, he bends to kiss her crooked mouth, and I am so close I can see how he twists his own lips to accommodate hers, and to show that her kiss still works.[3]

We are broken and wounded people. This side of heaven, we always will be. But there is no telling the power of words, mere words, to heal some of that brokenness—if they are as grace-filled and accommodating as that husband's kiss.

9

NEVER ON SUNDAY

If you call the Sabbath a delight
and the LORD's holy day honorable . . .
then you will find your joy in the LORD.

ISAIAH 58:13-14

he pain began as little stabs down the back of my legs. Since I was
running a lot at the time, preparing for my third marathon, I thought it
must be some kind of muscular stress, so I stretched more thoroughly before and after my workouts. But the pain got worse. Sometimes it would
wake me in the middle of the night. No matter what position I assumed,
it wouldn't go away. I practically wept with frustration and discomfort.

Finally I did what I should have done much earlier: I went to the doctor. He asked a few questions, manipulated my legs and sent me to get an
x-ray to confirm his diagnosis. Which it did. I had two herniated discs in
my lower back, as he had suspected. The doctor thought I might be able
to avoid surgery if I committed myself to six weeks of complete bed rest.
The "rest" actually took place on the floor because my bed was too soft.

I HAD CEASED

I was shaken and perplexed. My body had performed well for many
years; now it didn't. What did that mean for my future as a husband
and father, a man? And there was the church I had started three years

before: I was the entire pastoral staff. Who would preach? Who would lead the elders and plan the services? There was one positive in the six weeks' rest, I thought: I could read to my heart's content. But that didn't happen either, since the pain medication and muscle relaxant I was taking made me drowsy and my eyes unfocused. I read exactly one book in six weeks.

Mostly what I did at the beginning of those six weeks was hurt, worry and cry. The smallest thing would happen—a cross word, a morbid thought, even a telephone call from a well-wishing friend—and I would find tears running uncontrollably down my face. Walking was so painful that every trip to the restroom was a battle between my pain tolerance and the need to relieve myself. The pain sometimes won, and I'd have to lie down on the floor for a while to muster the strength to use the toilet. It was humiliating and emasculating. The worst was watching my sweet wife take on all the work of the household. We had two small children at the time—actually three, counting me—and she bore the brunt of their care. I couldn't do anything that mattered, it seemed: as a father and husband, as a pastor, as a provider, as an athlete, as a man. I had been shut down, stopped and stymied. I had ceased.

Then one day, about the third or fourth week of my ordeal, a thought dawned: I could pray. It didn't seem like a lot to me, but it was something. So I asked my wife, Lauretta, to get me a copy of the church directory. I purposed to pray through the entire membership every day, person by person. It usually took about two hours. It wasn't piety or a deep belief in the power of prayer that motivated me. If it had been, I would have prayed more when I was well. Instead, boredom and and a sense of impotence drove me to it. But soon the times of prayer became sweeter than any I had ever known. A new sense of intimacy with God and my people was emerging. The two hours flew by.

"STUPID"

I thought, *Wouldn't it be nice if I could keep this up once I was back to work?* One day near the end of my convalescence I said to God, "Father, I've enjoyed these times of prayer so much. It's too bad I won't have as much time to pray when I get back to work." His response was swift and blunt. He said, "Stupid." It was in a nice tone of voice, but that's what he said. "You have the same twenty-four hours when you are well as when you are sick," he continued. "The trouble with you is that when you are well you think you're in control; and when you are sick you know you aren't." Those words changed my life. Prayer has never been the same since, nor has the meaning of the words *cease* and *stop*.

"Cease" or "stop" is roughly the meaning of the Hebrew word translated "Sabbath" in the Bible. To cease or stop working one day out of seven is a command—one of the ten big ones, right up there with having no other gods or idols and not murdering. But like the rest, it is more than an order; it is a gift, a permission, even. Jesus goes out of his way to emphasize that the Sabbath was designed especially with humans in mind. "The Sabbath was made for man," he says, "not man for the Sabbath" (Mark 2:27). It is a command in the same way that joy is a command: we are ordered to follow it for our own happiness. "If you call the Sabbath a delight / and the LORD's holy day honorable / . . . then you will find your joy in the LORD" (Isaiah 58:13-14). Ideally we will choose to keep the Sabbath, but even when it is coerced as in my six-week cessation, it can be a blessing of incalculable worth.

Where not explicit, this idea is implicit throughout the Bible. For instance, Psalm 127 says it's no use building a house that the Lord is not building. It's worthless posting sentries around a city he's not protecting. It's the same with anxious and endless work: "In vain you rise early / and stay up late, / toiling for food to eat." Why is this so? Because the Lord "grants sleep to those he loves" (Psalm 127:2). In other words, if our work is our god, God won't bless it or us. For how can the true and living God bless a false god? But if God is God of our work, he will take care of us and the work. One of the ways we relinquish control to him is to cease work for his sake. The Sabbath is both a command and a permission, a demand and a gift, for he grants—and commands—rest to those he loves. Jesus said the same thing when he told us to cease all worry and seek first God's kingdom and his righteousness. Our worries will be taken care of, and we will be blessed (Matthew 6:25-34).

THE RHYTHM OF GRACE

What are the blessings of the Sabbath? The first is the obvious grace God gives when he says we not only must rest, but we may rest. One of the specific teaching passages on the Sabbath is Exodus 20:8-11. There the meaning of the Sabbath is linked to God's work of creation.

Remember the Sabbath day by keeping it holy. Six days you shall labor and do all your work, but the seventh day is a Sabbath to the LORD your God. On it you shall not do any work, neither you, nor your son or daughter, nor your manservant or maidservant, nor your animals, nor the alien within your gates. For in six days the LORD made the heavens and the earth, the sea, and all that is in them, but he rested on the seventh day. Therefore the LORD blessed the Sabbath day and made it holy.

The text tells us that God built a rhythm of work and rest into creation, into the very structure of the world. Break the rhythm and the melody goes bad. In the aftermath of the French Revolution, the Sabbath was abolished and replaced by one day of rest in ten. Voltaire reportedly said, "We cannot destroy Christianity until we first destroy the Christian Sabbath." But the experiment was a disaster: men and women crumbled under the strain and animals literally collapsed in the streets.

There is also a pattern to this rhythm: it moves not from work to rest, but from rest to work. The biblical day is not from sunup to sunup, as we reckon it, but from sundown to sundown. The days in the Genesis account of creation are measured:

And there was evening, and there was morning—the first day.
And there was evening, and there was morning—the second day.
And there was evening, and there was morning—the third day.

And so on, each day beginning with people lying down to rest. The pleasure of this pattern is easily verifiable. Compare how you feel on your day off if you begin it on the morning of the actual day instead of the evening before. If you had to work the evening before, you awake tired, don't you? You don't feel really rested and refreshed until noon, and then the day is half over. But if you begin it the evening before, you awake refreshed and ready to enjoy the whole day.

REST IS A NECESSITY

The pattern of creation is the same as the pattern of salvation. We move not from work to grace, but from grace to work—otherwise grace is not grace but wages. Paul's great words in Ephesians 2:8-10 capture this order neatly: "It is by grace you have been saved, through faith—and this not from yourselves, it is the gift of God—not by works, so that no one can boast. For we are God's workmanship, created in Christ Jesus to do good works, which God prepared in advance for us to do." There is the pattern: God saves us because of his grace. Salvation is his gift, not his reward for good work. But he gives us his grace so that we can work. As with salvation, so with creation: we don't work to receive grace; we receive grace to work. Rest is not a reward; it is a necessity. Joy!

The message of the Sabbath, then, is grace. If joy is what we experience when we are grateful for the grace given us, then keeping the Sabbath is a habit of joy. It reminds us that God is God and we are only people, and that is good. We can let him run the universe; all we need to do is find our place in his scheme. Work can press us down and bury us under its weight. But the Sabbath speaks grace into the lives of driven, harassed workers. It says to housewives and account executives, to welders and attorneys, "You may stop now—no, you *must* stop now—at least for a day."

The Bible also links the Sabbath to freedom. In the Sabbath commandment in Deuteronomy 5:15, the theological rationale is slightly different from the one in Exodus 20. The passage gives this explanation: "Remember that you were slaves in Egypt and that the LORD your God brought you out of there with a mighty hand and an outstretched arm. Therefore the LORD your God has commanded you to observe the Sabbath day." God is saying, "Once you were slaves and had to work or die. Now you are free. The Sabbath will ensure that you don't forget it. Stop working once a week to remember that you are free, not slaves."

AN ACT OF DEFIANCE

The Sabbath is therefore a freedom day; keeping it is an act of defiance and rebellion in a world enslaved to work. It is a weekly rebuttal of the worldly dogma that we justify our existence and sustain ourselves by achievement. The world says, "If you think nobody cares if you're alive, try missing a few car payments," and, "If you haven't got an ulcer, you're not carrying your share of the load." The command to keep the Sabbath holy empowers us to deflate all the imperial claims that work would make on our lives. It enables us to say, "No! I am not your slave! I'm stopping for the next twenty-four hours. In Christ I am free. My future well-being is in his hands, not in how well my hands serve you." Joy!

The beauty of the Sabbath is that it is a command. We would rarely rest if given the choice. We are like children who desperately need to take a nap but resist until we're exhausted. We need to be ordered by the Almighty to rest, or we'll keep obeying the orders of almighty work. There can be great delight in looking at a pile of tasks on the Sabbath and saying, "Not today. My Master says you'll have to wait until tomorrow."

Keeping the Sabbath doesn't mean that we don't attend to truly urgent matters. Jesus noted that if an ox fell into a ditch on the Sabbath, the law made provision for it to be pulled out. Sometimes things just happen on that day. But as Billy Graham commented, "If your ox keeps falling in a ditch on the Sabbath, you'd better fill in the ditch or tie up the ox." We need to order our lives so that we can stop at least one day a week without causing everything to come crashing down around us.

Some hear the Sabbath command as anything but an invitation to freedom. It sounds like one more thing to do in an already overextended life. And that's what it is, if keeping the Sabbath means doing in six days what we now do in seven. In that case, the Sabbath is a burden. There is no joy in it. Successful Sabbath keeping isn't about doing more work in less time or mastering new time management techniques. It is much more fundamental; it is a matter of repentance and conversion. It means renouncing a way of life that has no space for God and choosing, by faith, a life that does. Certainly there are techniques that a family can use to make keeping the Sabbath easier. Sabbath-keeping Jews can teach us a lot. But until this basic repentance and conversion take place, techniques are of no use. The real issue is, if you and I are too busy to stop working one day a week, then we are too busy, period. Our problem is sin, not lack of time. And we need to cry out for God's mercy.

A WINDOW TO THE FUTURE

The Sabbath is about grace, freedom and hope. Hope is implicit in the structure of the week in the Genesis account of creation. The story builds in a linear way from beginning to end—it doesn't endlessly repeat cycles but moves toward culmination, resolution, completion, consummation. In Judaism the week became a picture of history, of life lived toward the consummation, God's denouement of the human drama. The Sabbath became the high point of the week. For three days beforehand, the devout Jew looked forward to it. For three days afterward he looked back and savored what had been. God's eternal rest was the hope the Jew anticipated and out of which she lived.

For the Christian church, the Sabbath moved to Sunday because that was the day Jesus rose from the dead. In Christ the new life hoped for in Judaism was inaugurated by the resurrection. Now what had been lived toward was to be lived from, even though it was yet to be fully accomplished. The theme of hope is explicit in the New Testament: "There remains, then, a Sabbath-rest for the people of God; for anyone who enters God's rest also rests from his own work, just as God did from his. Let us, therefore, make every effort to enter that rest" (Hebrews 4:9-11).

The Sabbath is a window to the future. It points to a time when God will make sense of this mess. It hints at the eternal. It reminds us that there is meaning to our lives beyond the rat race. George Herbert wrote of the Sabbath:

> O day most calm, most bright,
> The fruit of this, the next world's bud.[1]

If it is true that a day of rest in this world is the "bud" of the world to come, then I can truly rest in hope the remainder of the week. The future is not in my hands but in God's, and this hope saves me from the hubris that gives my work idolatrous significance. If the Lord doesn't build the house, then whatever I do is in vain. But on the other hand, this hope also saves me from the despair that says nothing I do matters. Since the future is in his hands, he can take my labor and make it matter as he weaves it into his grand scheme of redemption and gives me my daily bread, to boot.

Take this hope out of work and joy quickly disappears as well. Our efforts become meaningless drudgery. C. S. Lewis's book *The Silver Chair* contains as apt an image of our times as I have ever read. When Jill and Eustace enter the underground world of the Witch, they discover there is no sun shining there, only dim, pale light revealing thousands of silent gnomes with blank faces, working. "Every gnome seemed to be as busy as it was sad, though Jill never found out what they were so busy about. But the endless moving, shoving, hurrying and the soft pad, pad, pad [of their feet] went on."[2]

A CATHEDRAL IN TIME

In the Sabbath we also gain time. What Jesus said about losing our life to find it (Mark 8:35) is true also of time. Remarkably, it is the time we give to God on this day that we get back. The logic here starts with the basic truth that just as God is Lord of all creation, he is also Lord of time. He uses the sun, moon and stars to mark off "seasons and days and years" (Genesis 1:14). He fills time with what he ordains, appointing a "season for every activity under heaven," including the exact minute of our birth and death. Every moment and every event we experience comes from the all-wise and all-loving hand of the Lord of time (Ecclesiastes 3:1-7).

The Sabbath is an emphatic reminder that God is the Lord of time. The Bible calls the Sabbath the Lord's holy day. The word *holy* means set apart for God, sanctified or consecrated; a day is a unit of time. Referring to the Sabbath as "the Lord's holy day" speaks of time set apart for God. To be sure, all our days are the Lord's, not just the Sabbath. But the Sabbath is designed to sanctify a part for the sake of the whole. Just as Christians are the salt of the earth, so the Sabbath is the salt of the week. We observe the Lord's Day not because this one day is the Lord's but because all days are the Lord's, and the Sabbath reminds us of that radical truth.

Here we come upon the great contrast between pagan religion and the faith of the Bible. Paganism concerned itself with the consecration of space. Above all, places were holy—nations and mountains, temples and groves. In the beliefs of the Canaanite peoples surrounding Israel in the Old Testament, the gods or Baals were gods of the earth and of agriculture.

But Judaism was "a religion of time aimed at the sanctification of time," writes Jewish theologian Abraham Heschel.[3] Certainly the temple, Jerusalem and the land God gave Israel were holy to the Lord. But before any of these, and after all these disappeared, Jews celebrated God's love and salvation with great days of feasting and rejoicing. If the temples of paganism were holy architectures in space, the Jewish holidays were holy architectures in time, with the Sabbath the chief structure.

According to Heschel, modern technical civilization is essentially pagan in its preoccupation with the conquest and manipulation of space—of things and objects. Moreover, technical civilization seems always to gain space at the expense of time. The more we have of things, it seems, the less we have of time. I am writing this book on a word processor that has cut by 40 percent the amount of time it takes me to complete a project. Has it saved me time? Not really. I now write twice as much as I used to. The net result is that I am busier now than when I had only a pen and a notebook.

But time, not space and things, is at the heart of our existence, says Heschel. Technical civilization looks for meaning in things; the faith of the Bible looks for meaning in time. For it was "when the time had fully come" that God brought us salvation in his Son (Galatians 4:4).

CHRONOS OR KAIROS?

The Bible's interest in the sanctification of time is best seen from the perspective of two Greek words. One is virtually absent from the Bible; the other is used almost exclusively in passages about time. The first is *chronos*. It refers to time from a quantitative, linear perspective. The second word is *kairos*, meaning time from the perspective of quality and meaning. To contrast the two, *chronos* means time as a dimension; *kairos* means time as circumstances. *Chronos* is a date; *kairos* is a season. *Chronos* is something to manage and control; *kairos* is something to understand and obey.

Which word do you think is used almost exclusively in the Bible? If you guessed *kairos,* you are correct. The Bible seems to be uninterested in time as *chronos* and concerns itself almost completely with time as *kairos.* Scripture places far more emphasis on the meaning of the time given us than the amount of time we have.

It's not hard to see which view of time prevails in our culture. We are a people obsessed with *chronos*—how to get more time, how to control and manage it. Some social analysts believe the invention of the clock has more radically affected the direction and shape of human civilization than any other event in the past five hundred years. Certainly our lives have been conditioned by the experience of wearing a wristwatch.

We are tremendously concerned with managing time, aren't we? We treat it as a substance to consume, and all we really do with our time management skills is find more things to do—more people to see, more projects to work on, more meetings to attend. And we wonder why we still feel spent and empty after all that managing. We assume we need help managing time because we are too busy. But the deeper issue is that we are too busy because we have lost a sense of the meaning of time.

How silly all this talk about time management seems from the perspective of the Bible—where time is understood as *kairos.* Time management. The notion is preposterous, even presumptuous. The Bible says we are to let *kairos* dictate to us what we will do and how we will live instead of the other way around. Paul uses the word *kairos* when he reminds the Christians in Rome to go about their days "understanding the present time" (Romans 13:11). He is urging them to be alert to the season in light of Christ's resurrection and return. To discern the *kairos* will mean to "behave decently, as in the daytime" (Romans 13:13). The Greek word translated "decently" in the New International Version carries nuances of elegance and grace. To really know the time is to live gracefully and elegantly—with class, if you will. It is to live as befits the season.

DO WE REALLY KNOW WHAT TIME IT IS?

The morning after my engagement to the woman who is now my wife, I was caught in a traffic jam with thousands of other men and women trying to get to work before their wristwatches said 8 a.m. The year was

1970 and my car radio was playing a popular song by the rock group Chicago. The lyrics described people rushing through a park on their way to work, wearing gold watches, and then asked, "Does anybody really know what time it is?" The song was implicitly about how *kairos* can be lost in *chronos*. That morning was one of the happiest of my life: the night before, I had heard the girl of my dreams tell me she would be my wife. I wanted to stop my yellow Volkswagen right in the middle of the freeway, stand on its roof and shout to the people locked in their cars around me, "Does anybody really know what time it is?"

When I look at our frantic pace, when I see how full we cram our lives with activities, most of them good, I question our concept of time. When I see how the Sabbath is just another day for doing what we do the rest of the week, I wonder if it is even possible for us to really believe and know that Christ is Lord of all, the beginning and the end, the one in whom we live and move and have our being.

We need the Sabbath to remind us what time it really is: the time between the resurrection of Jesus and his return to earth. The season is grace; the time is meant for deep gratitude and joy. We need the Sabbath to interrupt our *chronos* and point to the meaning of time so we can live with elegance and class. We need the Sabbath to remind us that since God is the Lord of time, we live by grace and not work, freedom and not slavery, hope and not despair.

In other words, as I discovered lying on the floor with my bad back, we all have the same *chronos* each day: twenty-four hours, no more, no less. We lack, however, a sense of *kairos*, the discernment to see what the time means and what God requires of us in it. That sabbath, as all sabbaths do, sensitized me beautifully to *kairos* and thus regained for me the time of which I never seemed to have enough.

The Sabbath says, "Stop. Look. Listen. Life is passing you by. The harder you run, the more you fall behind; the fuller you try to get, the more empty you become." Celebrate the Sabbath. Know that you live by grace. You are not a slave to necessity. You are free! Know that there is hope, that your life is moving toward a grand consummation, and that it will get there by God's doing, not your own. Stop. Look. Listen. Be joyful.

~10~

HILARIOUS GENEROSITY

If the landscape reveals one certainty,
it is that the extravagant gesture is the very stuff of creation.

ANNIE DILLARD

When Lauretta and I were first married, we were very poor. The three necessities of food, clothing and shelter weren't quite within our grasp. We could manage only two out of three—not bad as a batting average, but miserable if you're trying to live. My employment, if you could call it that, was selling swimming pools. The first six months we were married, I sold two. One Saturday morning the company I worked for asked me to drive down to Irvine, California, to pick up payment for a pool sold by one of the other salesmen. Since Irvine was near Newport Beach, Lauretta and I decided to make a day of it and have a picnic at the beach after I picked up the check.

The man who bought the pool was a Christian psychologist of the Pentecostal variety. You can read that both ways, for his psychology was as enthusiastic and Spirit-filled as his faith. At the time I found him a little frothy and tedious, but that said more about me than him. He was friendly and insisted that we come into his kitchen for a cup of coffee before giving us the check. As we sipped from our mugs, he launched into a discourse about the joys of tithing, giving 10 percent of one's income to the work of God's kingdom. At first I was puzzled at this conversational non sequitur, but I put up with it so we could get the check and get out. But as the minutes passed, I found myself feeling more and more like he had read my mind, or my mail. It had been years since I had given much to anything but my own whims and desires. I had felt vaguely uneasy about my selfishness, but now I was feeling something different. It wasn't guilt; it was more like longing, but for what? Had I been asked to name it I would have said I was longing for freedom.

After he wrote his check, he walked us out. As I was getting in my car, he touched my shoulder and said, "I hope you don't think I'm crazy or anything, but as I was praying this morning I felt the Holy Spirit telling me that I should talk to you about tithing." I mumbled something like, "That's okay," and shut the door. In truth my heart was pierced by what he had said. My lack of generosity extended to places beyond my pocketbook: I wouldn't even grant that the words he had spoken to me had any relevance to the condition of my life. That was years ago, and to this day I wish I could remember the man's name and tell him how my life was changed that day by what he told me. I think his last name was Rasmussen. If you ever read this, Mr. Rasmussen, I want to say thank you very, very much for listening to the Holy Spirit.

"FREEDOM'S JUST ANOTHER WORD FOR NOTHING LEFT TO LOSE"

As Lauretta and I drove down the Costa Mesa Freeway toward the Pacific Ocean, I asked her how she felt about what Mr. Rasmussen had said. She replied that she too was deeply touched. As we talked, we decided to make a go of tithing. But it wasn't just tithing that was at stake. We were really choosing freedom that day. We had been under pressure and duress for so long it was like we couldn't breathe, but now we could. So we couldn't afford food, clothing, shelter—so what? Had not Jesus promised that our Father in heaven would give us all we needed if we sought first his kingdom? I mean, we had done a pretty lousy job taking care of ourselves, right?

We decided to defy the law of grim necessity and give away what we did not have to others who needed money too. We would defy the received wisdom that God only takes care of those who take care of themselves. We would no longer be defined by our income, or lack of it. Our future would be in God's hands. I can still remember the place on the freeway where we made the decision. Gordon Lightfoot's version of "Me and Bobby McGee" was on the radio, and we knew it was playing just for us that day as we sang along: "Freedom's just another word for nothing left to lose." We laughed as we hadn't in a long time. Having nothing left to lose meant we had everything to gain.

The weeks that followed were just like stories I had read in Christian magazines. Somehow the money was always there. Once the amount we needed for rent appeared the day it was due, sealed in an envelope stuck in our mailbox. Another time we got a check for one hundred dollars, the exact amount we needed for car insurance. The friend who sent it wrote, "Don't pay me back when you are able. Instead, give it to someone else with the same stipulation." Later on that's exactly what we did. As far as I know, that hundred dollars is still traveling around the world. I feel a quiet gladness when I contemplate that possibility.

A CRAZY EQUATION

But that was only the beginning of the fun. We opened a separate bank account for the money we planned to give away, calling it our tithe account. We created it as a spiritual discipline to shield us from the temptation of "borrowing" from money we intended to give. The moment we received any income, we separated out the amount we'd covenanted with God to give, put it in the tithe account and kept it there until we wrote checks on it. Eventually 10 percent ceased to be the standard and became the point of minimum generosity, a place to begin, not end with. Every time we looked at the amount of money in that account, we felt richer. There it sat, totally at our discretion. We weren't poor anymore; we had money to give away!

And what fun it was to see a need, to feel an urging from God, and to give—just like that. More than once we giggled as we wrote a check, feeling like Mr. and Mrs. Santa Claus. We still have that account, and we're still having fun playing Mr. and Mrs. Santa Claus. And to be sure, we're still experiencing the delight of seeing God meet our needs through the generosity of others. Even now, Lauretta and I have been stunned by the way our church and friends have come to our side as we have brought my eighty-six-year-old mother into our home.

Freedom and fun. We were tasting a little bit of what some first-century Macedonians experienced, a crazy kind of equation. They were, I'm sure, much poorer than we were. But when they heard about the needs of Jewish Christians in Judea, and of the offering Paul was taking to relieve them, they pleaded for the privilege of giving. Really. Paul said of them, "Out of the most severe trial, their overflowing joy and their extreme poverty welled up in rich generosity" (2 Corinthians 8:2). That's the crazy equation: severe trial + extreme poverty + overflowing joy = rich generosity. Trial and poverty alone can't possibly equal generosity. But add joy to the mix and something miraculous happens. Minus one + minus one = more than ten thousand.

Where did the Macedonians' overflowing joy come from? From the place all joy comes from. It is what we experience when we are grateful for the grace given us. Gratitude answers grace like thunder answers lightning. Grace elicits gratitude like the voice of an echo. If we could fully see the grace shown us each day, no amount of gratitude or joy could possibly be excessive. No amount of poverty or trial could possibly squelch it. If love is as strong as death, as the Bible says it is (Song of Solomon 8:6), then the joy of genuine gratitude is stronger than the impulse to be stingy.

Paul explained the reason for the Macedonians' overflowing joy: "For you know the grace of our Lord Jesus Christ, that though he was rich, yet for your sakes he became poor, so that you through his poverty might become rich" (2 Corinthians 8:9). To fully take in the miracle of Christ's rich, overflowing generosity is to be changed forever. Grace equals gratitude equals joy. The greater the grace the greater the gratitude and joy, and the greater the power to transform misers into givers and trial into generosity.

NAKED ON THE STEPS OF THE CHURCH

The same kind of thing happened to a rich young brat named Francesco Bernadone in the thirteenth century. He stood naked one day before the whole city on the steps of the church, with nothing left to lose. His over-flowing joy had turned poverty and trial into freedom. The story of how he got there is wonderful—and pure gospel.

Francesco was the son of Pietro Bernadone, a rich cloth merchant who for years had indulged Francesco's boyish impulses toward wine, women, silly pranks and adventure. His friends were made of the same shallow stuff, and they called their fraternity "the Gay Brigade," a medieval version of "the Heartbreakers" or "the Party Animals." Their motto was "by wits or by fists." Any trouble they got into was swept under the rug and winked at as the natural overflow of youthful exuberance. Francesco was obsessed with the ideals of romantic chivalry and dreamed of gaining renown as a brave knight admired by men and adored by women. When his town went to war with its neighbor Perugia, Francesco got his chance. His father bought him the best armor and the best horse, and he rode off to battle.

Almost immediately, Francesco was captured by the enemy and tossed in jail. His daddy paid the ransom, bought him a new horse and armor, and sent him off again with a party and a page. But this time he never made it to the war. On his way he encountered a leper in the road. Disgusted, he dug his spurs into his horse's side to gallop by. But as he passed the leper, he saw Christ in him as "the least of these brothers of mine." He stopped, got off his horse and did something he never could have imagined before: he kissed the man's grotesque face, gave him alms, seated him on his horse and led him to his home. Years later Francesco, the man who became St. Francis of Assisi, wrote this about the incident:

> When I was in sin, the sight of lepers nauseated me beyond measure; but God himself led me into their company, and I had pity on them. When I had once become acquainted with them, what had previously nauseated me became a source of spiritual and physical consolation for me. After that I did not wait long before leaving the world.[1]

In other words, he was set free. He had set out for Perugia a well-dressed slave, imprisoned in armor, desperately needy for recognition and things, terrified of death and sickness—his own mortality. But he came home to Assisi a free man.

For a while, the young convert spent his time washing lepers' sores and praying in deserted churches. Once, while praying in a dilapidated chapel, he had a vision of the crucified Christ writhing in pain. In his agony, Jesus looked directly at him and spoke: "Repair my house which, as you can see, is falling into ruin." Francis took this literally and began immediately to repair the old building. To finance the project, Francis needed money. Thinking, perhaps naively, that his father would be as eager to help his son do good as he had been to help him do bad, he took a few bolts of Pietro's finest cloth, sold it and used the money for his chapel repairs. Pietro was appalled. Youthful exuberance was one thing; religious fanaticism was quite another. He had his son arrested and sued him for the money he had embezzled.

Thus the scene on the steps of the church: the whole town had turned out to witness the trial. Pietro disowned his son. Francis renounced his inheritance and gave the money back. The crowd gasped as he stripped off his clothes and threw them at his father's feet, for they had been made from his father's cloth. The stunned bishop spread his cloak over the naked Francis and pushed him into the church where he could find some rags in the poor box to cover him. Francis left Assisi singing.

GOD'S CLOWNS

Francis left Assisi alone, but he died with thousands of followers. The Franciscans, as they came to be known, ordered their lives according to the words of Jesus in Matthew 10:7-10: "As you go, preach this message: 'The kingdom of heaven is near.' Heal the sick, raise the dead, cleanse those who have leprosy, drive out demons. Freely you have received, freely give. Do not take along any gold or silver or copper in your belts; take no bag for the journey, or extra tunic, or sandals or a staff; for the worker is worth his keep." The Franciscans cared for the sick, played with children, preached the gospel in the vernacular to peasants and refused remuneration except for food to eat at the end of the day. Whatever was left over they gave to beggars or wild birds.

Some people called Francis *Pazzo*, or madman. He and his followers were having so much fun that they jokingly called themselves *Joculatores Domini*, or God's clowns. But they weren't the first to experience this kind of joy; before them were those crazy Macedonians, for instance. And Jesus could be considered the original clown, or all-time *Pazzo*. He is the one who said you'll find your life by losing it, for heaven's sake. Yes, for heaven's sake. "*Freedom's* just another word for nothing left to lose."

The joyous freedom of generosity is about much more than money. It's about how we see life. The joy of generosity is rooted deep in who we are as human beings created in God's image. We enter the world naked; we leave the world naked. The Lord gives; the Lord takes away; blessed be the name of the Lord (Job 1:21). That's about all there is for us. Everything we have is on loan: time, intelligence, strength, looks, friends and family—nothing belongs to us. The best things in life are free. Think about your life as I think abut mine.

I'll start with my birth, which like yours was remarkable. It was the biggest event of my life, the event without which there would be no other events—no school, no marriage, no children, no death. And yet I had absolutely nothing to do with it. I didn't plan it. I didn't ask for it. I did nothing to earn it. It was simply given to me. What followed was no different. For weeks and months I was wiped, washed, fed, cuddled and cared for. And I never even once said thank you. The things necessary for me to live were simply given.

Later on, as a young man of about thirteen, I made a rather unsettling discovery. There were girls in the world, and I was interested in them—in a positive way, that is. My interest was lively, and I wanted them to notice me too. I wanted one of them someday to love me and become my wife. But how? I had learned some valuable lessons up to this point. If I wanted to be a better athlete I could work harder. If I wanted to be a better student I could study harder. That was all simple and straightforward. But what could I possibly do if I wanted a woman to love me? Work harder? Try harder? At what? Being lovable? It was frightening to realize that skill and effort could take me only so far, and that this great thing I wanted I couldn't just go out and acquire. I could only receive it. When it came to love, I was completely at the mercy (a word I use with theological precision) of someone else. It would have to be a gift.

The best things that have happened to me have been just that: happenings. They aren't things I earned or planned or worked for. They are the givens, the gifts. The things that have given me the most joy in life are not things I deserved but things I didn't deserve. The Bible's word for this is *grace*. "Grace," writes Frederick Buechner, "is something you can never get but can only be given. There's no way to earn it or deserve it or bring it about any more than you can deserve the taste of raspberries and cream or earn good looks or bring about your own birth. A good sleep is grace and so are good dreams. Most tears are grace. The smell of rain is grace. Somebody loving you is grace. Have you ever tried to love somebody?"[2]

GOD DOESN'T CARE WHO HE IS NICE TO

According to the Bible, the fundamental truth of our existence, the base reality of the universe, is the inexplicable grace and generosity of God. Understood this way, grace is as primal to the creation of the world as it was to my birth. Woven into the fabric of the cosmos is the fact that God acted in sovereign and gracious freedom when he spoke it into existence. The creation is a free gift, extravagantly given. In fact, "If the landscape reveals one certainty," writes Annie Dillard, "it is that the extravagant gesture is the very stuff of creation."[3] When we are gratefully generous we are merely agreeing with the nature of existence, living according to the way things are.

There is more. God governs the universe with the same extravagant generosity he displayed when he made it. Case in point: as he governs he doesn't seem to care who receives his kindness. Jesus told us to love our enemies because it would make us like our Father in heaven. "He," said Jesus, "causes his sun to rise on the evil and the good, and sends rain on the righteous and the unrighteous" (Matthew 5:45). It's true. I can look out my study window at a beautiful day—blue skies, dazzling sunshine. And doggone it, the man who wrote me that nasty letter last year is probably enjoying the same beautiful day, right now, with me. God is indiscriminate, shamelessly so, in whom he shows his love to. It's not only his prerogative as God, it's his pleasure. He exults in saying, "I will have mercy on whom I will have mercy, and I will have compassion on whom I will have compassion" (Exodus 33:19).

Also—I say this by way of confession—it used to disturb me to see so many men and women outside the faith who were nicer than many inside the faith, myself included. Here is a gentle, kind, good-humored atheist or Muslim, and there is an ill-tempered, self-righteous prig of a Christian. Go figure. For the longest time, that contrast seemed to challenge the validity of the gospel. I think it was Nietzsche who griped that Christians would have to look a lot more redeemed before he would believe in their redeemer. I agreed. How could the gospel be true if so many non-Christians were more "Christian" than Christians?

Two insights helped me. One was a statement by a wise friend who said that when you see a Christian acting less than Christlike, remember that you have no way of knowing how bad he might be if he were not a Christian. You think she's awful now? Imagine how much worse she'd be if she didn't have the Holy Spirit. My friend was serious, and so am I. All who follow Jesus are on a journey, with some further down the road than others. And what about those "Christian" non-Christians? It's the same thing—the grace of God. They can no more take credit for the social and genetic factors that have made them who they are than we Christians can. It's all grace. God makes his rain fall and his sun shine on everybody: the good, the bad and the ugly. He created the world freely, by his grace. He governs it the same say. Even his worst enemies are recipients of his indiscriminate love.

BE HUMBLED

So again, when we are generous, we are not only acting in accordance with the nature of creation, we are imitating the God who governs creation—and who saves and redeems the world. Redemption is the best part of his generosity. The ugly nature of the human predicament is that we all are sinners who have fallen short of God's glory (Romans 3:23).

We have obstinately refused to live up to the glorious standard God set when he made us. Who knows better than our Creator what we were made to be? We do, we vainly imagine: we think we can be our own masters, be equal with God, even. But we turn out to be less than human in the attempt. The wages of this sin is death, and its root is ingratitude (Romans 6:23; 1:21).

What does God do with obstinate and ungrateful rebels who are dying because of their own sin? The same thing he did when he created them. He is generous; he graciously reaches out and actually seeks them (Luke 19:10). And his search takes him to death on a cross, given freely, whether or not those he seeks ever notice or care about his generosity. This is the definitive demonstration of his love, writes Paul: "While we were still sinners, Christ died for us" (Romans 5:8). This is generosity times infinity, grace virtually unheard of on a human level. The point is, you and I can do nothing to make God love us more than he already does and has. He already went to the limit. And nothing we do can make him love us less, because he loved us most when we were the least lovable. He isn't generous because we deserve it, for after all, it wouldn't be generosity if we did—it would be wages. He's generous because it's his character, his nature.

What do we do with all that divine generosity? The first thing we do is to let it put us in our place. We let it make us humble. Paul put a rhetorical question to a cocky bunch in ancient Corinth, and through divine inspiration he also directs it at us: "What do you have that you did not receive? And if you did receive it, why do you boast as though you did not?" (1 Corinthians 4:7). From God and to God and through God are all things, entirely on his own initiative, out of nothing, extravagantly and indiscriminately. We can give to God only what he first gave us. We're like the kid who wanted to give his dad a birthday gift, so he went to his father's closet, took a tie off the rack, wrapped it up and presented it to him with a "Happy birthday, Dad!" When we give to God, we take something wonderful that he has given and that belongs to him already, and we give it as though it was ours in the first place. And he is so kind, so gentle, this great God! He delights in the gifts we present, even though we couldn't give anything if he had not first showered gifts on us.

Only the humble can see the generosity that lies at the foundation of creation. For only they can get low enough. It is significant that our English word *humble* comes from the Latin root *humus,* which means earth. The humble are down-to-earth and, therefore, at just the right place to see things as they really are—to see the awesome grace that lies at the bottom of existence.

BE DAZZLED

When the humble see what only they can see, they are filled with wonder. That's the second thing we let God's generosity do: we let it impress us to the point of bedazzlement. King David looked at the miracle of grace that made him a human being and exclaimed in wonder, "Who am I?" He said to God, "When I consider your heavens, / the work of your fingers, / the moon and the stars, / which you have set in place, / what is man that you are mindful of him, / the son of man that you care for him? / You made him a little lower than the heavenly beings / and crowned him with glory and honor" (Psalm 8:3-5).

Our technology tends to cheat us of a sense of wonder. The greater the illusion that we have control over our world and, therefore, the "bigger" we feel, the less capable we are of this delightful sense of awe. A shrunken vision and atrophied imagination are the price we pay for our enlarged egos, writes Annie Dillard:

> An infant who has just learned to hold up his head has a frank and forthright way of gazing about him in bewilderment. He hasn't the faintest clue where he is, and he aims to learn. In a couple of years, what he will have learned instead is how to fake it; he'll have the cocksure air of a squatter who has come to feel he owns the place. Some unwonted, taught pride diverts us from our original intent, which is to explore the neighborhood, view the landscape, to discover at least where it is we have been so startlingly set down, if we can't learn why.[4]

This "unwonted, taught pride" makes us like the Texan who traded homes with a man from Colorado. When asked what he thought of Texas, the Colorado native said, "I don't like it; there's nothing to look at, just flat land as far as the eye can see." When asked how he liked Colorado, the Texan said, "I don't like it; there's nothing to look at, the mountains are in the way."

BECOME A HONEYCOMB

The third thing we let God's generosity do is mentor us. We let it make us imitators. Jesus says that when we are generous we are acting like children of our heavenly Father, loving with the same perfection he does (Matthew 5:44-48). When we are humbled and deeply impressed by what we see, the most natural response is to want to emulate it. My favorite singer/songwriter is Fernando Ortega. Every performance of his that I have attended has ended with a standing ovation by the audience. I have wondered sometimes what it would feel like to be ordered to keep silent after a concert, to be commanded not to express thanks. It would be painful! Restraint would abort my joy, somehow. Letting go to clap, shout and whistle allows my appreciation to be complete—almost. There is one thing left I can do to fully enjoy the gift: buy a CD and sing along. It is my way of imitating Fernando a bit.

In the same way, God's generous virtuosity is meant to call forth the highest compliment we can give: to try to be like him, to give him glory and be glorified ourselves in the imitation. There are three kinds of givers. Some are like flint: they must be hammered to give anything, and then all that comes forth is sparks and chips. Some are like sponges: they must be squeezed to give anything, but the moment the squeezing stops, the water goes right back in. Some are like honeycomb: they ooze sweetness because of what they've become inside.

Those crazy Macedonians had become honeycombs because of what they had come to know of God. As Paul wrote of their overflowing joy and rich generosity, he used the word *grace* in a rather fluid way. Grace was what they had received from Jesus (2 Corinthians 8:1). Grace was also their ability and desire to give—"the grace that God has given the Macedonians" (2 Corinthians 8:1). And the giving was itself a grace

(2 Corinthians 8:7). They received grace, they became gracious, and their graciousness led to more grace. Grace was all around, creating a veritable riot of goodness and gladness that helped the cycle continue.

The Macedonians help us understand that the practice of generosity positions us to receive more grace. Or to use Paul's metaphor, generosity plants seeds of grace that grow into more grace: "Remember this: Whoever sows sparingly will also reap sparingly, and whoever sows generously will also reap generously" (2 Corinthians 9:6). Generous sowing is such a powerful means of grace that it will bring a bumper crop of joy, an "overflowing in many expressions of thanks to God" (2 Corinthians 9:12).

Our Father God loves it when his children try to act like him. He loves a cheerful giver (2 Corinthians 9:7). The Greek for *cheerful* is the word behind our English word *hilarious*. All translations that I know of opt for the word *cheerful* over *hilarious*. I'm sure the scholars have sound exegetical reasons for doing so. But I opt for *hilarious,* not for exegetical reasons but for experiential ones. That's the way it is: broke, self-absorbed young marrieds become Mr. and Mrs. Santa Claus; a spoiled brat becomes a saint and a clown; poor Macedonians become big-time spenders; Pentecostal psychologists become prophets. Hilarity abounds.

PART THREE

THE HOPE OF JOY

Hope is hearing the music of the future.

Faith is to dance to it.

RUBEM ALVEZ

ᔰ 11 ᔱ

HEAVEN

Our Real Home

*There have been times when I think we do not desire heaven
but more often I find myself wondering whether, in our hearts,
we have ever desired anything else.*

C. S. LEWIS

*W*ell done, thou good and faithful servant. . . . Enter . . . into the joy of thy lord" (Matthew 25:21 KJV). All my life I have longed to hear God speak these words. So have you, whether or not you know it. They are the sweetest, most joyous words a human can ever hear, for to enter into the joy of the Lord is to enter the reality of which all other joys are but shadows, or counterfeits. To live in this joy is what all living has been for. It is to come home to heaven.

The hope of heaven has been terribly misunderstood, however. Some regard it as an opiate for the masses,[1] a narcotic to dull the oppressed to the sting of injustice and to soothe the uneasy consciences of people who could do something about it. The hope of "pie in the sky, by and by," of deferred celestial pleasure, has been used to keep slaves in their place. The hope of heaven has also been called mercenary, causing people to believe that holiness and righteousness have no great value in themselves but are merely means to an end. Eternal bliss is a balloon payment at the end of a life of moral exertion. Further, a secular culture and a secularized church see heaven as irrelevant or implausible. "Almost all of our modern philosophies," writes C. S. Lewis, "have been devised to convince us that the good of man is to be found [only] on this earth."[2]

WHAT IS THE GOAL OF IT ALL?

But the hope of heaven's joys is essential not only to Christian faith but also to the meaning of human existence. According to philosopher Immanuel Kant, there are three great questions of ultimate importance:

What can I know?
What should I do?
What may I hope?

The Bible's answer to "What can I know?" is that we can trust the Word of God. "What should I do?" is answered by the command to love God with our whole being and our neighbor as ourself. Hope in heaven is the Bible's answer to the last question, "What may I hope?" This last question is at least as important as the first two, for it includes other big issues: Why am I alive? What is the purpose of existence? What is the meaning of it all?

It is amazing what people can endure as long as they know why they have to endure it. That is what the hope of heaven has meant to Christians through history. To die to self, take up one's cross and follow Christ has never been easy (Luke 9:23-24). The Christian church has frequently been persecuted, and obeying Christ has cost believers their jobs, social standing and lives. Almost every Christian has had moments when he wondered if the price of believing was worth the reward. The old aphorism of virtue being its own reward takes us only so far. The law of diminishing returns sets in as the pain of practicing virtue rises. There has to be more if we are to sustain the long obedience that is the Christian life. Only the perspective of heaven can make the trials and afflictions of this life seem "light and momentary," transcended by "an eternal glory that far outweighs them all" (2 Corinthians 4:17).

What will heaven be like? It is hard to say—not because of its uncertainty, but because of its glory. The only subject that strains human language more than heaven is the God of heaven, for indeed, "No eye has seen, / no ear has heard, / no mind has conceived / what God has prepared for those who love him" (1 Corinthians 2:9). It really can't be described, but I'm going to try anyway—in the hope that my feeble efforts will stir a hunger for the indescribable and spur you on to trust in Jesus, the Way to heaven (John 14:6).

GOD'S APPLAUSE

In heaven we will be congratulated by God. That is the thrust of Jesus' parable about the faithful stewards, who will hear their master say, "Well done. . . . Come and share your master's happiness" (Matthew 25:14-23). The triumphant, martyred saints in John's vision of heaven, dressed in white robes and waving palm branches, are receiving their congratulations (Revelation 7:9-17). White robes are the first-century equivalent of tuxedos and black ties. The saints' dress is formal, symbolizing victory and honor along with the palm branches. "These are they who have come out of the great tribulation" (Revelation 7:14). God is pleased with them, and they themselves could not be more pleased that he is.

These glorified saints are experiencing the distinct pleasure an inferior receives when congratulated by a superior.[3] This pleasure isn't like Rembrandt enjoying my compliments of his painting *The Prodigal Son,* but me enjoying his praise of my little watercolor still life. It isn't like Luciano Pavarotti hearing me clap after an aria, but him cheering me as I sing in the shower. The need to be praised by those we admire, to please those we hold high, runs deep in us. It is one of the strongest motivators of human behavior. From childhood on, we crave the praise and attention of parents and friends. With it we flourish; without it we wither.

I've known many workaholics in my life, people driven to exhaustion and exasperation by their compulsion to achieve. One man I know stopped in his tracks when his long-suffering wife said to him, "Your dad is never going to come see you play baseball. Please stop trying to make him." All his life he had hungered for his father's approval but never received it. Unconsciously, he looked for it everywhere he could, as a student and an athlete, then as a professional. Nothing could fill up the hole inside. He was like Buechner's glutton, raiding the refrigerator to cure a case of spiritual malnutrition.[4]

GOD IS SATISFIED

Much as we esteem masters like Rembrandt and hunger for recognition from our fathers, these examples are microscopic compared to the idea of receiving honor from the Almighty. All the opinions of everyone in the world don't add up to God's. Heaven is the place where we will finally be congratulated by the Greatest. Having the hope of his praise in our hearts imparts something of the joy of heaven before we reach heaven. "God is easy to please, but hard to satisfy," wrote George MacDonald.[5] He is the perfect father none of us have had, or been. Like a good parent who cheers when his eighteen-month-old child tries her first steps, or manages a spoonful of food in her mouth and not on her face, he is delighted with our tiny efforts toward holiness. He is easy to please.

But like a good parent, he will not be satisfied until we walk and run as adults. His relentless love will pursue us with his holy demands until we are all he made us to be. To know the delight of the Heavenly Father in this life is the sweetest of all pleasures. But to know the satisfied pleasure of God in heaven is to know joy indescribable. To have finished the race, fought the good fight and kept the faith—and then to receive the crown of righteousness from a satisfied righteous Judge (2 Timothy 4:7-8)—how can I describe the joy? I love to pray the prayer of Dora Greenwell:

> And O, that He fulfilled may see
> the travail of His soul in me,
> And with His work contented be.[6]

This is the best I can do with this wonderful truth. I pray God will open your eyes to the "hope to which he has called you, the riches of his glorious inheritance in the saints" (Ephesians 1:18).

WE APPLAUD GOD

In heaven God is worshiped continuously. The book of Revelation is filled with scenes of saints engaged in endless worship throughout eternity. The supreme reward of those who have gone through the great tribulation, having their robes washed white in the blood of the Lamb, will be to serve God "day and night in his temple" (Revelation 7:15). They render the service of priests, engaging in never-ending worship before the throne of God.

"Is that it?" That was my first thought when, as a twelve-year-old middle school student, I noticed this feature of heaven's "joys." Up till then, I had thumbed through Revelation to relieve my boredom sitting in worship services at my church. Its monsters and bloody descriptions of cosmic conflict was the closest I could get to a superhero comic while being forced to sit in a pew in those days. But then I realized that the very thing I was trying to escape by reading Revelation was actually what Revelation was all about: the eternal worship of Almighty God. Suddenly *Star Wars* turned into an interminable performance of Handel's *Messiah*. At age twelve, this seemed a fate only slightly better than going to hell. I was appalled and a little disgusted. Would this be my reward for serving Jesus? I went to my Sunday school teacher and demanded an explanation. He assured me that I need not worry; all those scenes of worship in heaven were "only" symbolic. I took that to mean that whatever heaven was, it would be better than worship. Though not completely satisfying, this explanation held my misgivings at bay through middle school, high school, college, seminary and the first few years of ministry.

However, though I was not conscious of it, something was changing in me over those years: my mind and heart were expanding in their appreciation of the glory of God. As God became grander to me, my experience of worship got better. A new thought emerged: suppose I read one of Shakespeare's sonnets to my dog—what would be his response?[7] At first he would wag his tail and sniff the book in my hand to see if it were edible. Then he would lose interest in the book and my voice. He's only a dog, right? He hasn't the capacity to appreciate great literature.

But what would it mean if, as I read to him, he perked up his ears, looked at me with bright eyes and barked his approval? I could only conclude that something miraculous had happened to his nervous system and that he had been given the gift of appreciating the literary masters. The question is, would Shakespeare's sonnet be any greater because my dog liked it? No, of course not. Would my dog be greater? Yes!

What I didn't understand as a youth was that my problem with worship was *my* problem. God wasn't boring; I was. I lacked the spiritual and mental capacity to enjoy him. Perhaps heaven's most delightful prospect is that our humanity will be glorified in a way that lets us see and appreciate God fully; we'll realize that nothing could be sweeter than simply to gaze at him and sing our approval. God won't be better because we appreciate him, but we will. "We know that when he appears, we shall be like him, for we shall see him as he is" (1 John 3:2). Beholding is becoming. "The glory of God is man fully alive," wrote the church father Irenaeus. Then he added, "The life of man is the vision of God." God is never more glorified than when a human being made in his image comes fully alive. But we don't come fully alive until we see God as he really is.

INTIMACY WITH GOD

In heaven we will know unparalleled intimacy with God. The hope of heaven is that "he who sits on the throne will spread his tent over them" (Revelation 7:15). This passage is an allusion to the exodus, when the tent that housed the Holy of Holies symbolized God's presence with his people. Only the appointed priest could stand in this privileged place in the presence of God. But in heaven this intimacy is opened to all God's people when he spreads his tent over them and covers them with his presence. When this happens we will be welcomed into the heart of reality itself.

We've all had hints of this reality along the way, small tastes of what is to come. In the summer of 1975 my wife, Lauretta, and I hiked the trail that runs along the crest of the Grand Tetons in Wyoming. As we walked north, toward the Grand Teton peak itself, we could look below to the east and west and see one hundred miles into Wyoming and Idaho. The view was unforgettable; it seemed we were seeing all we would ever want to see in life. But what took our breath away was the

Grand peak. It knifed its way into the sky through the clouds that clung to its summit. Its beauty and power made us ache inside, sweetly.

Why did we experience this exquisite longing? There were two reasons.[8] One was the pain of separation: we were looking at something that powerfully drew us in but that we could not enter. In fact, the closer we got to the mountain, the more its beauty seemed to elude us, withdraw and disappear. The other was the pain of loneliness. We were drawn to something that gripped and controlled our attention but that paid no attention to us. You could say we were "in love" with something that didn't even know we existed.

But suppose the mountain had spoken to us as we stood there gazing at it in longing and loneliness? Suppose it had said, "Hello, Ben and Lauretta. I have known you from all eternity. I want you to be with me. Come closer to me; come into me and be as close as you can while remaining yourselves." That is heaven's reward for those who have gazed faithfully and adoringly at God here on earth. It is the fulfillment of Paul's prayer that we be filled to the measure of all the fullness of God (Ephesians 3:19). For to be in God is to be of God, to actually "participate in the divine nature" (2 Peter 1:4), and still be human.

DRINK FROM THE FOUNTAIN OF JOY

In heaven we will also know strong desire and deep satisfaction. There is a curious paradox in Revelation 7. On one hand the text says there will be no more hunger or thirst in heaven: "Never again will they hunger; / never again will they thirst" (Revelation 7:16). We will be filled and satisfied. On the other hand it says the Lamb, the Lord Jesus Christ, will be our Shepherd and "lead them to springs of living water" (Revelation 7:17). Though satisfied we will still drink; though filled we will want more. I think there is here a picture of the deepest joy and pleasure. Think of how it would be to be always hungry and always filled at the same time. Think of how great it would be to enjoy food the way we do when we take our first hungry bite, and to be as peaceful and satisfied as when we take our last. For me, the saddest part of any great meal is the moment when I want no more: it's over and done, I've had enough, the initial delight is unsustainable. Okay, I know I enjoy food more than most people and more than I probably should. But are not all pleasures enjoyed in the anticipation as much as in the partaking? Is it not sad when both are over? Is it not our curse to sometimes want joy but not have it, or to have it but not want it, to lose the capacity to know and appreciate what we've been given?

Here's a story that attempts to illustrate these ideas. Twenty-five pounds and twenty years ago, when I was still a runner, a friend and I entered a 10K race at a park in Southern California. The location of the event was near the junction of three freeways, which is to say it was an extremely smoggy place. Why we entered that particular race I'm not sure. Maybe it was to get the T-shirt that said we'd run 6.2 miles. Maybe it was because we naively thought there would be minimal air pollution early on a Saturday morning. Whatever our reasoning, by the time the race started the air was hot and toxic. But I was hopeful: I had trained hard and was set to run the fastest 10K of my career.

The race began and I was running well, I thought. But when I got my first split (the time announced at the first mile) I was running slower than ever. So I stepped up my pace. The second split had me running even slower than the first. This was terrible! By the fifth split, I was exhausted and apparently running at a snail's pace. As I neared the end of the race, I heard a lot of cursing ahead—the closer I got, the more profanity filled the air. When I crossed the finish line of the slowest 10K I had ever run, I found out why so many of my fellow runners were upset. The distance had been mismeasured and was nearly eight miles instead of 6.2! No one knew just how far off the splits had been. The T-shirt was lousy too.

My friend Ralph and I were tired and dehydrated, so our first stop on the way home was for lunch. We ordered a pitcher of our favorite carbonated beverage and poured two glasses. We each took a long swallow. I felt the cold liquid go down my throat into my esophagus and into my stomach—I could feel the shape of my stomach from the delightful sensation the drink produced as it swirled around there. Ahhh. We looked knowingly at each other. "Was it worth it, Ben?" Ralph asked. Good question. Was it worth it to struggle through so much frustration and deprivation just to experience that first swallow? I didn't hesitate. I said, "Yes!"

I believe that in some way we can only dream of now, in a manner that this illustration only barely touches, we will spend eternity drinking from the fountain of joy and saying to each other, "Was it worth it?" Without hesitation we will answer, "Yes!"

Each and Every Tear

Here's one more aspect of eternity in God's presence. In heaven we will be healed. The Bible doesn't say there will be no tears in heaven, but it does say that "God will wipe away every tear from their eyes" (Revelation 7:17). I know many people for whom the greatest gift would be the grace to weep. Their wounds are so deep and covered by fear and lies that right now they can only be silent. Their cries are choked off. For them, tears must come before praise.

I know a Ugandan man who built an orphanage after Idi Amin's reign of terror ended and he was allowed back into his country. The orphanage was filled with children who had seen their parents tortured and murdered. Many had suffered unspeakable abuse themselves. The orphanage's founder said that, strangely, none of the children ever wept. They had suffered so long and so hopelessly that tears were useless. They had grown cold and hard inside. This man and his staff loved and cared for the children the best they could, and then one day a breakthrough came. Two children were fighting over a toy. One hit the other in the face, wrested the toy from her hands and ran off. The little girl burst into tears—and the staff of the orphanage rejoiced! The healing had begun; the child could cry.

The sense of the Greek in Revelation 7:17 is strong singular. God will wipe away every tear, each and every tear, every single tear, each one. The picture is one of tenderness, like the evening when one of my small children fell down and scraped his chin on the sidewalk. I held him in my arms and told him I was going to wipe away each and every tear on his cheek. The faintest hint of a smile broke through; he liked the idea.

So with great deliberateness I wiped each tear from his cheek, one by one. When I finished, I asked him, "Is it better now?" He solemnly pointed to a tear on his face and said, "You missed one, Daddy." When I wiped it away he grinned, then laughed, and then jumped off my lap and went to play.

Will heaven be like that? Infinitely better, no doubt. But a little like it, I believe. God misses nothing that comes to us because it must pass through his heart first. The One who heals the brokenhearted is also the One whose heart was broken.

THE GIGANTIC SECRET

In one of his most pregnant sentences, G. K. Chesterton wrote, "Joy which was the small publicity of the pagan is the gigantic secret of the Christian."[9] In other words, the mass of people have been forced to be happy about little things and sad about big ones. For the pagan, things like death and eternity are terrors to be denied, dismissed or stoically accepted. The only things left to be happy about are small and transitory, such as health, money, friends, houses and vacations. Even the higher pleasures of the mind last only as long as the mind, which is not long in the grand scheme of things. Plato's joys ended for Plato when Plato ended. This is contrary to the very nature of joy, says Chesterton. "Joy ought to be expansive, but for the agnostic it must be contracted; it must cling to one corner of the world"—the here and now. Grief, however, is expansive, he says, for its "desolation is spread through an unthinkable eternity."[10] The most the pagan can do with this miserable state of affairs is to create publicity for the little things. We see this "much ado about nothing" in the way we inflate language, describing the trivial in terms that apply only to God: "awesome" tacos, "ultimate" fitness centers, cars called "Infiniti."

Chesterton said this was like being born upside down: head in the abyss, feet dancing in the air. "To the modern man the heavens are actually below the earth. . . . The explanation is simple: he is standing on his head, which is a very weak pedestal to stand on."[11] To be converted is to be set right side up, feet placed squarely on the ground, head in the heavens, "eyes wide open to the mercies of God."[12] With the head unstuck, the feet can walk the earth—they can dance. Have you ever heard that someone was "too heavenly minded to be any earthly good"? Really, the only way to be any earthly good, and to know joy, is to be heavenly minded.

The gigantic secret of the Christian is that joy is truly expansive, as big as God's grace and as eternal. Grief is a mere interlude, a kind of waiting room, a staging area on the outskirts of eternal joy. Things may be awful now, but the here and now is passing away, never to return. Our joy springs from a deep thankfulness that "our light and momentary troubles"—and all troubles are just that—"are achieving for us an eternal glory that far outweighs them all. So we fix our eyes not on what is seen, but on what is unseen. For what is seen is temporary, but what is unseen is eternal" (2 Corinthians 4:17-18).

One September when I was serving as dean of the chapel at Hope College in Holland, Michigan, a first-year student was tragically killed in a biking accident. His name was Ben Buckout. Strangely, it seemed at the time, he and his father had biked together to college from their home in Minneapolis. All that distance had been no trouble, then a short ride around town and the young man was dead. But I came to believe that God in his mercy gave a father and his son that particular gift before they were parted.

The Buckout family had a robust faith and blessed the whole college with their witness to hope in the resurrection. The father was especially courageous and clear about that hope. A year later he came back to speak to the student body. He told of attending a band concert the spring after his son's death. Ben had played in the band and had a special affection for the spring performance. As Mr. Buckout sat in the auditorium that evening, he was overwhelmed with grief as he listened to the music. He half-thought, half-prayed, "Ben, if you could only see this!" Then, he told us, it was as if he heard Ben's voice answer, "Dad, if you could only see this!" Amen and amen.

The bereaved and broken have experienced this kind of assurance innumerable times in the history of the church. Tears of grief and joy come from the same place—the place where the tragedy of human existence meets the miracle of God's grace. Grief for the Christian is real and can be savage. But it is only an interlude. Joy is the truly expansive thing.

WELCOMED INTO A CITY THAT HAS
LONG AWAITED MY ARRIVAL

As discussed earlier, Kant's fundamental question "What may I hope for?" is of ultimate importance because it deals with the purpose of life. If we know why we are alive and where we are headed, we can cope with whatever comes along. Pain, loss, disappointment and any number of other joy busters take on a different hue when seen from the perspective of the end of the journey. Though the joys of heaven are "inexpressible and glorious," they may fill our hearts and set our feet moving to the tunes of the future even now. They tell us we are in fact receiving the goal of our faith, which is the salvation of our souls (1 Peter 1:8).

There are times when I feel a deep sadness just before I fall asleep at night. I can hear the gentle breathing of the woman I love sleeping beside me. I think of the four wonderful young adult children we so respect and delight in. I think of the beautiful and exceptional college I serve at, of its students, staff and faculty. I think of friends and burritos and New York strip steaks and music. Life is excruciatingly good! The more deeply I appreciate it, the sadder I feel as I see it slipping away. I can't hold on to any of these things; I can only receive them with gratitude and someday release them—hopefully with the same gratitude. But whether gratefully or not, I will release them. I will die.

Either this life we live is an absurdity of incomprehensible proportions, or it is in the care of a loving God who pledged himself to us in the resurrection of Jesus and promises us the hope of heaven. I believe this hope is the deepest longing of every human heart. It is the desire for our true home, the home that cannot fade, "the city with foundations, whose architect and builder is God" (Hebrews 11:10). This hope is the source of our deepest joy, the reality that makes us fundamentally sound, whatever the circumstances.

Sometimes I indulge a little fantasy when I get off an airplane in a strange airport and no one is there to greet me. I imagine that someone will show up unexpectedly and that I will be surprised by a familiar voice calling out, "Hey, Ben!" I will be embraced and welcomed into a city that has long awaited my coming, even though I didn't know it.

One day I will arrive at that strangest of destinations we call death. A voice will call out and say, "Hey, Ben! Well done, good and faithful servant. Enter now into the joy of your Master." And I will be welcomed into a city that has long awaited my coming. I will be congratulated and expanded and glorified and healed and led into that "great story, which no one on earth has read; which goes on forever: in which every chapter is better than the one before."[13] All that came before was just the title page. Joy! Inexpressible!

≈ 12 ≈

GLORIOUS FREEDOM

*In my opinion whatever we may have to go through now
is less than nothing compared with the magnificent future God has
planned for us. The whole creation is on tiptoe to see the wonderful sight of
the sons of God coming into their own. . . . And the hope is that in
the end the whole of created life will be rescued from the
tyranny of change and decay, and have its share in
that magnificent liberty which can only
belong to the children of God!*

ROMANS 8:18-19, 21 (PHILLIPS)

I lived in Southern California for the first forty-seven years of my life.
But on September 24, 1989, I packed up my family and left home to pastor a church in New Jersey. As the jet plane made the big circle out of Los Angeles International Airport, over Marina Del Rey and the Pacific Ocean, I wondered where our belongings were, somewhere down below in a moving van between California and New Jersey. I looked at my precious wife and our little family: four kids ages twelve, nine, seven and five. I looked at our one-way tickets to New Jersey. We had no plans to return, we didn't know what was ahead, and I was more than a little scared. Like most Americans, I am a provincial; leaving the Southwest for the Northeast felt like falling off the edge of the planet.

I felt for the first time a little of what the Bible means when it says,

"All these people were still living by faith when they died. They did not receive the things promised; they only saw them and welcomed them from a distance. And they admitted that they were aliens and strangers on earth" (Hebrews 11:13). What had been home was no more; what would be home was yet to be seen.

JOY: WHAT WE EXPERIENCE WHEN WE ARE GRATEFUL

The last chapter was about a home not yet seen—heaven, our real home, our eternal dwelling. There was a song about heaven we used to sing in the Baptist church where I grew up:

> O Lord, you know I have no friend like you;
> If heaven's not my home, then Lord what will I do?
> The angels beckon me from heaven's open door,
> And I can't feel at home in this world anymore.

Thoughts of heaven should make us homesick for our home not yet seen—and joyful! Heaven is one of the reasons joy is commanded in the Bible. God knows we can choose joy because he has given us compelling reasons to be thankful, and joy is what we experience when we are grateful for the grace given us.

That simple formula has been the burden of this book. It is illustrated by the relationship between three Greek words with the same root, *char,* which has to do with health or well-being. Grace is *charis,* gratitude is *eucharistia,* and joy is *chara.* It works like this: God pours out his grace on us in countless ways—in creating us, preserving us and, above all, redeeming us. What else can we do but be grateful? "How can anything more or different be asked of man?" writes Karl Barth. "The only answer to charis is eucharistia. . . . Grace and gratitude belong together like heaven and earth. Grace evokes gratitude like the voice of an echo. Gratitude follows grace like thunder lightning."[1] And as gratitude follows grace, so joy follows gratitude, for joy is the impact of the thunder of gratitude.

BRILLIANT, LUMINESCENT HUMANNESS

The pattern is repeated throughout Scripture: God does something

wonderful and people praise and thank him joyfully. What else could
they do—praise him somberly? apathetically? morosely? Genuine gratitude is necessarily joyful. The greater the grace, the greater the gratitude; the greater the gratitude, the greater the joy.

The promise of heaven is a huge grace and a huge reason to be thankful and therefore joyful. Heaven is our destiny with God, through faith
in Jesus Christ. The implications of being human completely and eternally in God are staggering. In a word, it means glory. God wants nothing
less than for us to share in his glory. In ways we can now only imagine,
he desires that we become as brilliant and luminescent in our humanness as he is in his Godness, splendid and magnificent and holy. A cho-
rus of New Testament voices speaks of this glorification beginning with
Jesus, who says that "the righteous will shine like the sun in the kingdom
of their Father" (Matthew 13:43). His apostles say the same thing:

> Paul: "And we, who with unveiled faces all reflect the Lord's glory,
> are being transformed into his likeness with ever-increasing glory,
> which comes from the Lord, who is the Spirit" (2 Corinthians
> 3:18). "For our light and momentary troubles are achieving for us
> an eternal glory that far outweighs them all" (2 Corinthians 4:17).
> "That you may be filled to the measure of all the fullness of God"
> (Ephesians 3:19).

> Peter: "He has given us his very great and precious promises, so
> that through them you may participate in the divine nature"
> (2 Peter 1:4).

> John: "Dear friends, now we are children of God, and what we will
> be has not yet been made known. But we know that when he ap-
> pears, we shall be like him, for we shall see him as he is" (1 John
> 3:2).

What so scandalizes and disgusts the devils in C. S. Lewis's *The
Screwtape Letters* is God's intention for people. "One must face the fact
that all the talk about His love for men and His service being perfect
freedom," Screwtape writes Wormwood, "is not (as one would gladly

believe) mere propaganda, but an appalling truth. He really does want to fill the universe with a lot of loathsome little replicas of Himself— creatures whose life, on its miniature scale, will be qualitatively like His own, not because He has absorbed them but because their wills freely conform to His."[2]

THE WEIGHT OF GLORY

The Hebrew word for glory, *kabod,* means "weight." So God's glory is his weight, quite literally. When Paul spoke of "an eternal glory that far out-weighs them all" (2 Corinthians 4:17), he was thinking of this Hebrew word and describing a weight that is more substantial than any earthly trouble. God's glory is not God himself but the impact, the "weight" of who he is. His glory is like the steps of the tyrannosaurus rex in the movie *Jurassic Park.* When the creature drew near, its footsteps shook the earth. Only with God, his weight is his holiness.

The impact of God's glory on people has always been something like what Jacob Needleman observed at the launch of Apollo 17 in 1975. The launch was at night, and a bunch of cynical reporters were milling about cracking jokes and drinking beer as they waited for liftoff. But every-thing changed when the countdown for the launch began. Needleman described it:

> The first thing you see is this extraordinary orange light, which is just at the limit of what you can bear to look at. Everything is illu-minated with this light. Then comes this thing slowly rising up in total silence, because it takes a few seconds for the sound to come across. You hear a "WHOOOOOSH! HMMMMM!" It enters right into you.
>
> You can practically hear jaws dropping. The sense of wonder fills everyone in the whole place, as this thing goes up and up. The first stage ignites this beautiful blue flame. It becomes like a star, but you realize there are humans in it. And then there is total silence.
>
> People just get up quietly, helping each other up. They're kind. They open doors. They look at one another, speaking quietly and

interestedly. These were suddenly moral people because the sense of wonder, the experience of wonder, had made them moral.[3]

But God's weight involves much more than wonder, as powerful as that wonder is. His glory is the splendor of his holiness and the weight of his absolute love and goodness. To be near his glory is either to be crushed and destroyed or changed forever. And to be changed is to become glorious.

IT IS ENOUGH

There are two dimensions to God's grace. On one level he simply accepts us as we are, unconditionally, when we profess faith in Christ. "God demonstrates his own love for us in this: While we were still sinners, Christ died for us" (Romans 5:8); "For it is by grace you have been saved, through faith—and this not from yourselves, it is the gift of God" (Ephesians 2:8). These truths alone are transforming, life-changing. The simple knowledge that you are loved and accepted by God can break into your life with startling luminosity. It reminds me of a day I was in the gym with my son, working out with weights. "Pumping iron" is weighty and can feel glorious. The rush of endorphin-packed blood into the muscles is one of life's underrated pleasures. On that day I was sweating and huffing and puffing, rock and roll music was blaring, and metal plates were slamming against bars. I was totally absorbed in the experience. As I loaded the bench-press bar for my son, I heard him mutter something that got lost in the din. I shouted, "What did you say?" He blushed and muttered it again. "Speak up, I can't hear you!" I shouted as I adjusted the weights. He blushed again, and spoke just loud enough to be heard: "I said, 'I love you, Dad.'"

Time seemed to stop and the music and commotion of the gym faded into the background as I realized that my son had been watching me and loving me. It took my breath away. I don't remember anything else that happened that day, whether good or bad. But whatever the day had been, those four words spoken amid the clatter of the gym were enough to set everything right and put the world back into perspective. It wasn't just the words; it was who said them that made them matter. My beloved son said them, and it was enough.

It is enough to believe that our glorious God has spoken his love to us and said, "I accept you and forgive you." God knows how we humans come alive in trust. He should; he made us that way. He also knows how we wilt when there is no trust. Think of it for a moment on a purely human level. Do you know people who, when you are around them, make you feel like you're at your worst? I can think of a person right now who, it seems, always looks at me through squinty, critical eyes. My belief is that he regards me as oafish, shallow and arrogant. I can't prove that he sees me that way, but my experience has led me to believe, right or wrong, that he does. So how do I act when I am around him? To my great frustration and embarrassment, I often find myself saying and doing things that are, in fact, oafish, shallow and arrogant. The harder I try not to be what he thinks I am, the more I end up behaving in just that way.

I'm reminded of my experience in middle school baseball. I had a bad reputation as a baseball player—richly earned, I might add. I just couldn't get the eye-hand coordination thing down. In later years, my success as an athlete would mainly come in games where I could knock people over. But baseball required finesse. Fly balls would come my way and I would miss them by a foot, or if they hit my hands, they bounced out. I was always the last player chosen for teams at recess or after school. It got so bad that when someone hit a ball my way, my teammates immediately started screaming at me not to drop it. My drop rate rose with the screams. Sometimes the ball would hit me on the head or in the face. It was humiliating. I wasn't a good baseball player to begin with, but I got worse with harsh criticism. I wilted under mistrust.

The truth is, I am a sinner. Whether I'm with my critical friend or not, I do have a capacity to be oafish, shallow and arrogant—a great capacity. But it gets bigger when I'm around him. I sink to fulfill his opinion of me, or what I believe to be his opinion of me. I wilt under mistrust.

On the other hand, I know a few people whose presence makes me flourish, and I'll bet you do too. When I'm with these people I'm wiser, funnier and smarter. You should see how great I can be when I'm with my wife, for instance. To this day, after thirty-three years of marriage, I still feel I overmarried. I really do. My wife believes such pleasant fictions about me! But when I am with her, those fictions become nonfictions. She knows my faults: my oafishness, shallowness and arrogance. But she nevertheless thinks I am a wonderful husband and father and a delightfully funny and wise man. Nevertheless! What an amazing word of grace it is. My wife's "nevertheless!" frees me to say "nevertheless!" too.

God's love works that way on our humanity. When we hear and believe the word of grace he speaks to us, we are freed to become more glorious, more holy, more righteous. We are given the right, as John puts it in his gospel, to become children of God (John 1:12); we are given the power to act like him. A new identity produces new behavior.

To Be Changed Is to Become Glorious

But more is at work here than psychology. The other dimension of God's grace is his supernatural power to change us. His acceptance and forgiveness in Christ, like the word I heard from my son that day in the gym, is a word he speaks to us. When God speaks a word, it is more than a mere sound or idea; it is him going out and creating reality. He says, "Let there be light" (Genesis 1:3) and there is light. His word goes out from his mouth and accomplishes what he desires (Isaiah 55:11). To hear God say, "You are forgiven" is to be forgiven and changed. "The word is near you," wrote Paul, "the word of faith we are proclaiming: That if you confess with your mouth, 'Jesus is Lord,' and believe in your heart that God raised him from the dead, you will be saved" (Romans 10:8-9).

Paul said this word is like the power that raised Jesus from the dead. In fact, the apostle actually prayed that this supernatural power would be at work in the Ephesian believers. In two remarkable prayers, he prayed that they would

> know the hope to which [God] has called you, the riches of his glorious inheritance in the saints, and his incomparably great power for us who believe. That power is like the working of his mighty strength, which he exerted in Christ when he raised him from the

dead. . . . I pray that out of his glorious riches he may strengthen
you with power through his Spirit in your inner being, so that
Christ may dwell in your hearts through faith . . . that you may be
filled to the measure of all the fullness of God. (Ephesians 1:18-20;
3:16-17, 19)

I've memorized these prayers and pray them often for myself and others. They are shining examples of the glory God intends for his children
to share with him.

HIS LABOR TO MAKE US LOVABLE

But God's power to change us involves more than his acceptance of us,
as wonderful as that is. God loves us just as we are, but he loves us too
much to let us stay that way. His love is "love to the loveless shown, that
they might lovely be."[4] His love is a holy love, "a consuming fire" (Hebrews 12:29), and his command is "be holy, because I am holy" (1 Peter
1:16). God is holy and we are not. But his love wills to make us holy. "To
ask that God's love should be content with us as we are is to ask that God
cease to be God," wrote C. S. Lewis in *The Problem of Pain*. "Because he
is what he is, his love must, in the nature of things, be impeded and re-
pelled by certain stains in our present character, and because he already
loves us he must labor to make us lovable. We cannot even wish, in our
better moments, that he should reconcile himself to our impurities."[5] So
God's holy love "may forgive all infirmities and love still in spite of them:
but Love cannot cease to will their removal. Love is more sensitive than
hatred itself to every blemish of the beloved. . . . Of all powers he forgives
most, but he condones least: he is pleased with little, but demands all."[6]

When he became a Christian, George MacDonald thought of his life
as a house that needed repairs. The roof was leaking, the porch was sag-
ging and the toilet overflowed; he had a bad temper, a lust problem and
a few other vices growing like weeds in the garden. He expected Jesus to
make the necessary repairs. But Jesus didn't repair anything—he tore the
house down, dug up the foundation and began all over again. Jesus' goal
is not to remodel but to rebuild. He wants us to be glorious, not so-so.

We can easily misunderstand this part of God's character as unrealistically perfectionistic, complaining that his demands are those of a cosmic martinet and only a select few, if any, can meet them. His call to holiness and perfection may sound like the callous "fitness" tests that were once given to immigrants at Ellis Island. Though thousands of immigrants entered the United States at Ellis Island in the nineteenth and early twentieth centuries, some were turned back soon after they arrived. The United States government did not want the feeble-minded, tubercular, or those with lung disease or glaucoma to enter the country. Doctors would determine who had bad eyes or lungs or who was mentally handicapped by having all immigrants walk up several flights of stairs to an examination area.

I'm physically fit, but when I visited Ellis Island and climbed those stairs, I was out of breath at the top. In those days doctors would stand at the top of the stairs to see who was stumbling and wheezing or otherwise laboring to make it up. These individuals would be pulled out of the crowd, away from their families, and sent back to the boats. It was heart wrenching to see. Spiritually, it can seem that God is a doctor scrutinizing us from the top of the stairs, and we are all blind and tubercular, struggling and stumbling our way to failure. Who can possibly be holy as he is holy?

But imagine one of those doctors spying a man coughing and wheezing his way up the stairs, blind and groping for help. The doctor runs down the stairs to the man, picks him up and helps him the rest of the way to the examination area. Then he administers food and antibiotics and checks him into a hospital, personally covering all his expenses. When the man is released, the doctor takes him into his home and includes him as a member of his family. That would be like God. The demand is still there: health remains a requirement. But with the requirement comes the means to meet it.

All of these truths come together in one of the classic biblical texts on God's grace, Ephesians 2:8-10.

For it is by grace you have been saved, through faith—and this not from yourselves, it is the gift of God—not by works, so that no one can boast. For we are God's workmanship, created in Christ Jesus to do good works, which God prepared in advance for us to do.

God's gracious acceptance is a gift, received through faith, pure and simple. But once received, his grace works in us as holy love. God's grace is also power to make us what he intended from the beginning: his "workmanship, created in Christ Jesus to do good works, which God prepared in advance for us to do." The requirement remains, but with it comes the means to meet it.

Augustine understood this grace when he prayed, "Give what you command, and command whatever you want." This was the promise prophesied in Ezekiel: "I will give you a new heart and put a new spirit in you; I will remove from you your heart of stone and give you a heart of flesh. And I will put my Spirit in you and move you to follow my decrees and be careful to keep my laws" (Ezekiel 36:26-27). It is the grace celebrated by the psalmist who prayed, "I run in the path of your commands, / for you have set my heart free" (Psalm 119:32).

God's desires for us are bigger and better than the best we can imagine for ourselves. He wants nothing less for us than glory, but we glom onto glory substitutes, imitations of the heavenly throne Jesus promised we will share with him in glory. Read the promise in Revelation 3:21. It will blow your mind and blow away all the fakes. Take popularity, for instance. "Popularity?" wrote Victor Hugo, "It's glory's small change."[7] The same can be said of all the other imitations. Fame, sex, ambition, money—they're all glory's small change.

SHINING LIKE THE SUN

What do you want out of life, a throne or a cheap imitation? That question brings us back to the one posed at the beginning of this book: Does God think we want too much or too little? I'll let C. S. Lewis give the answer again:

If we consider the unblushing promises of reward and the staggering nature of the rewards promised in the Gospels, it would seem that our Lord finds our desires not too strong, but too weak. We are half-hearted creatures, fooling about with drink and sex and ambition when infinite joy is offered us, like an ignorant child who wants to go on making mud pies in a slum because he cannot imagine what is meant by the offer of a holiday at the sea. We are far too easily pleased.[8]

Hopefully by now your standards have been raised and you are no longer satisfied with anything less than glory and joy inexpressible.

What will we be like when we are glorious? To describe it we can only grope with the images and metaphors of Scripture, being aware of the limits of human language. Jesus said, "The righteous will shine like the sun in the kingdom of their Father" (Matthew 13:43). What can that mean? Will the brightness of our humanity be like what the sun is to other light—so much brighter that we'll have to squint to look at each other? Is what we are now, the reflection of God in our humanness, a match flame compared to what we will be?

Think of the way the sun dominates the sky and provides the gravitational center of the solar system, of how the planets reflect its light and all living things depend on it for sustenance. Does Jesus mean that our glorification will have the same characteristics as the sun in the solar system? Will our freedom mean its freedom too? Perhaps Paul's words in Romans 8 are another way of expressing the same thing: "The whole creation is on tiptoe to see the wonderful sight of the sons of God coming into their own. . . . And the hope is that in the end the whole of created life will be rescued from the tyranny of change and decay, and have its share in that magnificent liberty which can only belong to the children of God" (Romans 8:19, 21 Phillips).

We will discover that when we are set right, everything else will be set right too. Consider the possibilities—some based on Scripture and some my own speculation: Babies will put their hands in cobra dens and not be harmed. Lion and lamb will lie down together, and the lamb will get a good night's sleep. We will discover that the Dr. Doolittle stories were not just fantasy, and in our freedom animals will talk human, or humans will talk animal. The trees really will clap their hands for joy, and we will hear the music of the spheres. The highest mountains, the deepest oceans and the densest forests will become home to us. The farthest reaches of the universe will be ours to touch and explore—all because we have finally realized the full implications of what it means to be human. The possibilities are dazzling, like the sun.

THERE ARE NO ORDINARY PEOPLE

Whatever the truth of my musings, we can be sure of this: When we see Jesus we will be like him, the "radiance of God's glory" (1 John 3:2; Hebrews 1:3). This hope purifies us, the Bible says (1 John 3:3). And even though we don't see it yet, it fills us with "an inexpressible and glorious joy," because we know that we are receiving the goal of our faith, the salvation—the glorious freedom—of our souls (1 Peter 1:8-9). This hope and its joy should change forever the way we see others and ourselves, knowing as we do that

> the dullest and most uninteresting person you talk to may one day be a creature which, if you saw it now, you would be strongly tempted to worship. . . . There are no ordinary people. You have never talked to a mere mortal. Nations, cultures, arts, civilization—these are mortal, and their lives are to ours as the life of a gnat. . . . Next to the Blessed Sacrament itself, your neighbor is the holiest object presented to your senses.[9]

Over the years in my work as a pastor, I have often looked into people's eyes as I served them the Blessed Sacrament, or Communion. It is one of the most precious and moving things I do in my calling. Sometimes as I serve the bread and the cup and repeat the words of Jesus, "Take and eat; this is my body, broken for you. Drink this in my memory; it is my blood, poured out for you," I think I see in their faces something of their glory to come. After all, in ways I believe no Christian tradition has fully explained, Jesus offers his life to us in the sacrament. He wants to be in us as intimately as food put in our mouths, chewed, swallowed and digested—to become part of the molecular structure of our bodies. Is there not glory unimaginable and joy inexpressible in the offer, "Take and eat; drink this"? He wants us to be in him, and himself to be in us. He said, "I have told you this so that my joy may be in you and that your joy may be complete" (John 15:11).

One Saturday afternoon in a large stone cathedral in Europe, the sexton was making final preparations for the organ to be played the next day in the Sunday services. Thinking the door was locked, he was startled to hear footsteps in the sanctuary. He turned to see a man in tattered traveling clothes walking down the aisle in his direction. The stranger greeted him briefly, but his eyes were on the organ. He fumbled nervously with the hat in his hand, then said to the sexton, "I've traveled a great distance to see this organ. Would you be so kind as to open its console so I could look at it for a moment?"

The sexton answered, "The organist is very particular, sir. He would be furious if anything on the organ were not working perfectly tomorrow. I must refuse your request."

But the traveler pressed the sexton, assuring him that he knew organs well and would be careful not to damage it. The sexton agreed to let him look in the console.

The traveler asked, "Could I please sit on the bench?"

The sexton hesitated, then replied, "Only for a moment."

The traveler sat on the bench for a moment, and asked, "Could I play just a few bars?"

The sexton felt trapped. "Only a few bars, then you must leave."

The traveler began to play, and lovely music filled the cathedral, more beautiful than any the sexton had ever heard. The traveler played for several minutes, then stopped, scooted off the bench and thanked the sexton for his generosity.

The sexton said, "Thank you! The music was gorgeous. May I ask your name, sir?"

"Felix Mendelssohn," the traveler answered, and walked away.

The sexton watched one of the greatest organists and composers of the nineteenth century walk out the door and thought, "Just think; I almost kept the master from playing his music in my cathedral."

The master's music is the hinge on which the door to joy swings. Will you let Jesus in to play his music and make you glorious—to fill you and expand you to the measure of all the fullness of God? For in his presence there is joy and eternal pleasure forevermore (Ephesians 3:19; Psalm 16:11).

NOTES

Introduction: We Are Far Too Easily Pleased

[1]Cited in Robert Short, *The Parables of Peanuts* (New York: Harper & Row, 1968).

[2]C. S. Lewis, *The Weight of Glory* (Grand Rapids, Mich.: Eerdmans, 1977), pp. 1-2.

[3]G. K. Chesterton, *Orthodoxy,* vol. 1 of *The Collected Works of G. K. Chesterton* (San Francisco: Ignatius Press, 1986), p. 365.

[4]Cited in Virgil Hurley, *Speaker's Sourcebook of New Illustrations* (Dallas: Word, 1995), p. 44.

[5]Blaise Pascal, *Pensées,* trans. A. J. Krailsheimer (New York: Penguin, 1983), p. 133.

[6]Frederick Buechner, *Telling the Truth* (San Francisco: Harper & Row, 1977), p. 81.

[7]J. R. R. Tolkien, quoted in Buechner, *Telling the Truth,* p. 81.

[8]Isaac Loeb Peretz (1852-1915) was a Polish Jewish writer of great distinction in the late nineteenth and early twentieth century. The story as I tell it is embellished somewhat but is faithful to the events as Peretz told in his short story, originally titled *Bontsche Shveig.*

[9]Augustine, *The Confessions,* trans. Edward Bouverie Pusey (Chicago: Encyclopaedia Britannica, 1952), p. 1.

Chapter 1: Inexpressible and Glorious Joy

[1]Frederick Buechner, *Wishful Thinking* (New York: Harper & Row, 1973), p. 34.

[2]Karl Barth, *Church Dogmatics* 4/1, *The Doctrine of Reconciliation* (Edinburgh: T & T Clark, 1980), p. 41.

[3]Told by Robert J. Morgan in *On This Day* (Nashville: Thomas Nelson, 1997), reading for May 25.

[4]Blaise Pascal, *Pensées,* trans. A. J. Krailsheimer (New York: Penguin, 1966), p. 309.

[5]Blaise Pascal, *Pensées,* p. 152.

[6]Peter Kreeft, *Christianity for Modern Pagans* (San Francisco: Ignatius Press, 1993), p. 304.

[7]George MacDonald, *George MacDonald, An Anthology by C. S. Lewis* (New York: Macmillan, 1947), p. 42.

[8]George Herbert, "Gratefulnesse," in *The Temple* (London, 1633).

Chapter 2: Joy Busters

[1]John Steinbeck, *East of Eden* (1952; reprint, New York: Penguin, 1992), p. 9.

[2]Horatio Spafford, "When Peace Like a River," *The Hymnal for Worship and Celebration* (Waco, Tex.: Word Music, 1986), p. 493.

[3]William Cowper, "God Moves in a Mysterious Way," in *The Hymnal* (Philadelphia: Presbyterian Board of Christian Education, 1933), p. 103.

[4]Quoted by John Piper, *The Roots of Endurance* (Wheaton, Ill.: Crossway, 2002), p. 57.

[5]R. C. Sproul, "We've Grown Accustomed to His Grace," *Preaching Today,* transcript of tape no. 88 (Carol Steam, Ill.: Christianity Today, 1990).

[6]Thomas à Kempis, *Prayers from the Imitation of Christ,* ed. Ronald Klug (Minneapolis: Augsburg, 1996), p. 22.

Chapter 3: The Happy God

[1]Quoted in Eugene H. Peterson, *A Long Obedience in the Same Direction* (Downers Grove, Ill.: InterVarsity Press, 2000), p. 95.

[2]Clifton Fadiman, ed., *The Little, Brown Book of Anecdotes* (Boston: Little, Brown & Co., 1985), p. 371.

[3]From a biographical sketch of the life and work of Jonathan Edwards, by Phillip E. Howard, in the introduction to *The Life and Diary of David Brainerd,* ed. Jonathan Edwards (Grand Rapids, Mich.: Baker, 1989), p. 14.

[4]Annie Dillard, *Pilgrim at Tinker Creek* (New York: Harper's Magazine Press, 1974), p. 9.

[5]Blaise Pascal, *Pensées,* trans. A. J. Krailsheimer (New York: Penguin, 1983), p. 201.

[6]Quoted in Daniel Fuller, *The Unity of the Bible* (Grand Rapids, Mich.: Zondervan, 1992), pp. 123-24.

[7]C. S. Lewis, *Surprised by Joy* (New York: Harcourt, Brace & World, 1955), p. 229.

[8]John Piper, *Desiring God: Meditations of a Christian Hedonist* (Portland: Multnomah Press, 1986), p. 116.

[9]G. Frederic Bergin, ed., *Ten Years After: A Sequel to the Autobiography of G. Müller* (London: J. Nisbet, 1906), pp. 152-54.

[10]Bernard of Clairvaux, "Jesus, Thou Joy," in *Hymns II,* ed. Paul Beckwith, Hughes Huffman and Mark Hunt (Downers Grove, Ill.: InterVarsity Press, 1976), hymn 27.

Chapter 4: A Christmas Carol

[1]*The Heidelberg Catechism* (Grand Rapids, Mich.: CRC Publications, 1975), p. 9.

[2]Ibid.

[3]C. S. Lewis, *God in the Dock and Other Essays* (Grand Rapids, Mich.: Eerdmans, 1970), pp. 243-44.

[4]Clifton Fadiman, ed., *The Little, Brown Book of Anecdotes* (Boston: Little, Brown & Co., 1985), p. 543.

[5]Blaise Pascal, *Pensées,* trans. A. J. Krailsheimer (New York: Penguin, 1983), p. 133.

[6]Paul Brand, *In His Image* (Grand Rapids, Mich.: Zondervan, 1984), pp. 235-36.

[7]This is an adaptation of a statement by Pascal: "In the perspective of these infinities, all finites are equal." *Pensées,* p. 93.

[8]Quoted in "To Illustrate," *Leadership Journal* (Fall 1984): 54.

[9]Robert Lowry, "Here is Love," traditional, sung by Fernando Ortega on *Night of Your Return* (Randolph Productions, 1996).

[10]I commend to you Piper's two marvelous expositions of joy, *Desiring God: Meditations of a*

Christian Hedonist (Portland: Multnomah Press, 1986) and *The Pleasures of God: Meditations on God's Delight in Being God* (Portland: Multnomah Publishers, 2000).

[11]Charles Dickens, "A Christmas Carol," in *Christmas Stories* (Chicago: M. A. Donohue, n.d.), pp. 67-68.

[12]Ibid., p. 69.

Chapter 5: Indiscriminate Thanks

[1]James Hewitt, ed., *Illustrations Unlimited* (Wheaton, Ill.: Tyndale, 1988), p. 264.

[2]Quoted in Robert Llewelyn, *Our Duty and Our Joy* (London: Darton, Longman and Todd, 1993), p. 1.

[3]I am indebted to Old Testament scholar Tremper Longman III for this aphorism and insight given during a lecture at a men's retreat.

[4]Thomas Merton, *Thoughts in Solitude* (New York: Farrar, Straus & Cudahy, 1958), quoted by Bob Benson and Michael W. Benson, *Disciplines for the Inner Life* (Waco, Tex.: Word, 1985), pp. 335-36.

[5]Rubem Alves, *Tomorrow's Child: Imagination, Creativity, and the Rebirth of Culture* (New York: Harper & Row, 1972), p. 195.

[6]Virginia Stem Owens, *And the Trees Clap Their Hands: Faith, Perception, and the New Physics* (Grand Rapids, Mich.: Eerdmans, 1983), quoted in Bob Benson and Michael W. Benson, *Disciplines for the Inner Life* (Waco, Tex.: Word, 1985), p. 334.

[7]George Herbert, "The Elixir," in *The Complete Works of George Herbert,* ed. Alexander B. Grosart (New York: AMS, 1983), p. 212.

[8]Quoted in Llewelyn, *Our Duty and Our Joy,* p. 1.

Chapter 6: Knowledge Too Wonderful

[1]Peter Taylor Forsyth, *The Soul of Prayer* (Grand Rapids, Mich.: Eerdmans, 1910), p. 14.

[2]Thomas Howard, *Hallowed Be This House* (New York: Ignatius Press, 1979), pp. 115-16.

[3]George Herbert, "Providence," in *The Complete Works of George Herbert,* ed. Alexander B. Grosart (New York: AMS, 1983), p. 133.

[4]Ibid.

[5]I am paraphrasing Rubem Alves, *Tomorrow's Child* (New York: Harper & Row, 1971), p. 195.

[6]In the 1970s a theologian with whom I have deep differences wrote a book called *Apology for Wonder.* Great title, lousy book. As bad as the book was, however, he was right about its premise: We need to allow ourselves to be dazzled. The word *apology* is from the Greek *apologia,* meaning "a defense, a case for."

[7]From John Gross, ed., *The Oxford Book of Aphorisms* (Oxford: Oxford University Press, 1984), p. 70.

[8]George Herbert, "Evensong," in *The Complete Works of George Herbert,* ed. Alexander B. Grosart (New York: AMS, 1983), p. 61.

Chapter 7: How Good and Pleasant

[1]Eugene Peterson, *A Long Obedience in the Same Direction* (Downers Grove, Ill.: InterVarsity Press, 2000), p. 175.

[2]Peter Taylor Forsyth, *The Soul of Prayer* (London: Independent Press, 1954), p. 11.

[3]Frederick Buechner, *Wishful Thinking* (New York: Harper & Row, 1973), p. 88.

[4]W. Norman Pittenger, *Praying Today: Practical Thoughts on Prayer* (Grand Rapids, Mich.: Eerdmans, 1974), posted on Religion Online, ed. Ted and Winnie Brock <www.religiononline.org/showchapter.asp?title=2292&C=2222>.

[5]Blaise Pascal, *Pensées,* trans. A. J. Krailsheimer (New York: Penguin Books, 1983), p. 309.

[6]Ibid., pp. 309-10.

[7]Peter Kreeft, *Christianity for Modern Pagans: Pascal's Pensées Edited, Outlined and Explained* (San Francisco: Ignatius Press, 1993), p. 321.

Chapter 8: Words That Give Life

[1]C. S. Lewis, *The Screwtape Letters* (New York: Macmillan, 1944), pp. 53-54.

[2]Edythe Draper, ed., *Draper's Book of Quotations for the Christian World* (Wheaton, Ill.: Tyndale, 1992), p. 653.

[3]Richard Selzer, *Moral Lessons: Notes in the Art of Surgery* (New York: Simon & Schuster, 1976), pp. 45-46.

Chapter 9: Never on Sunday

[1]George Herbert, "Sunday," in *The Complete Works of George Herbert,* ed. Alexander B. Grosart (New York: AMS, 1983), p. 84.

[2]C. S. Lewis, *The Silver Chair* (New York: Macmillan, 1953), p. 127.

[3]Abraham Heschel, *The Sabbath* (New York: Farrar, Straus & Giroux, 1957), p. 8.

Chapter 10: Hilarious Generosity

[1]Quoted in James Cowart, *People Whose Faith Got Them into Trouble* (Downers Grove, Ill.: InterVarsity Press, 1990), p. 45.

[2]Frederick Buechner, *Wishful Thinking* (New York: Harper & Row, 1973), pp. 33-34.

[3]Annie Dillard, *Pilgrim at Tinker Creek* (New York: Harper's Magazine Press, 1974), p. 9.

[4]Dillard, *Pilgrim,* pp. 11-12.

Chapter 11: Heaven: Our Real Home

[1]Karl Marx's beliefs regarding religion still have wide appeal in Western intellectual circles.

[2]Quoted in Peter Kreeft, *Heaven: The Heart's Deepest Longing* (San Francisco: Harper & Row, 1980), p. 16.

[3]C. S. Lewis wrote a brilliant exposition of this idea in his book *The Weight of Glory* (San Francisco: HarperSanFrancisco, 2001).

[4]Frederick Buechner, *Wishful Thinking* (New York: Harper & Row, 1973), p. 31.

[5]Quoted in Peter Kreeft, *Fundamentals of the Faith* (San Francisco: Ignatius Press, 1988), p. 194.

[6]Dora Greenwell, "I Am Not Skilled to Understand," in *Hymns II,* ed. Paul Beckwith, Hughes Huffman and Mark Hunt (Downers Grove, Ill.: InterVarsity Press, 1976), hymn 101.

[7]As with so many insights, I am indebted to C. S. Lewis for this thought, though I don't remember where I read it.

[8]This insight comes from C. S. Lewis's essay "The Weight of Glory," in *The Weight of Glory* (Grand Rapids, Mich.: Eerdmans, 1977), pp. 1-15.

[9]G. K. Chesterton, *Orthodoxy,* vol. 1 of *The Collected Works of G. K. Chesterton* (San Francisco: Ignatius Press, 1986), p. 365.

[10]Ibid.

[11]Ibid., pp. 364-66.

[12]J. B. Phillips's paraphrase of Romans 12:1, of life lived "in view of God's mercy." *The New Testament in Modern English* (London: Geoffrey Bles, 1960).

[13]C. S. Lewis, *The Last Battle* (New York: Macmillan, 1956), p. 174.

Chapter 12: Glorious Freedom

[1]Karl Barth, *Church Dogmatics* 4/1, *The Doctrine of Reconciliation* (Edinburgh: T & T Clark, 1980), p. 41.

[2]C. S. Lewis, *The Screwtape Letters* (New York: Touchstone, 1996), p. 41.

[3]Quoted in "To Illustrate," *Leadership Journal* (Summer 1995): 93.

[4]Samuel Crossman, "My Song Is Love Unknown," in *Hymns II,* ed. Paul Beckwith, Hughes Huffman and Mark Hunt (Downers Grove, Ill.: InterVarsity Press, 1976), hymn 61.

[5]C. S. Lewis, *The Problem of Pain* (New York: Touchstone, 1996), p. 45.

[6]Ibid., p. 41.

[7]Edythe Draper, ed., *Draper's Book of Quotations for the Christian World* (Wheaton, Ill.: Tyndale, 1992), p. 209.

[8]C. S. Lewis, *The Weight of Glory* (Grand Rapids, Mich.: Eerdmans, 1977), p. 2.

[9]Ibid., p. 15.

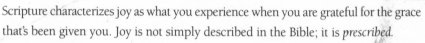

THE CHRISTIAN *GOSPEL* IS ABOUT GRACE.
THE CHRISTIAN *LIFE* IS ABOUT GRATITUDE AND JOY.

Scripture characterizes joy as what you experience when you are grateful for the grace that's been given you. Joy is not simply described in the Bible; it is *prescribed.*

Still, there's plenty going on in the world and in our own lives to make joy seem impractical, gratitude unnecessary and grace perplexing. We who have been given every reason to be joyful can nevertheless be so joyless. How can we begin to live in the joy of the Lord?

With gleeful exuberance, Ben Patterson submits his compelling case for joy. His winsome stories and thoughtful reflections show how even traditional practices such as churchgoing and (gulp!) tithing can be hilariously fulfilling when lived out of gratitude for God's gracious gift.

"If anything seems clear about most Christians today, it is that we have lost the peculiar joy that Jesus promised no one could ever take away from us. But perhaps this is not the joy we've been seeking. Ben Patterson points us back in the biblical direction of that unspeakable joy we were made to inhabit that longs to inhabit us."

MICHAEL CARD, *songwriter, musician and author of* **A Fragile Stone**

"There were so many wonderful things I loved reading in this book—Mary singing her song into the darkness; Dos Equis Dave and the brown-suited pastor driving around in the VW; Pascal, Herbert, Lewis, the Scriptures. Ben Patterson makes it all work together beautifully as he urges the Christian to make a habit of joyfulness."

J. FERNANDO ORTEGA, *musician and songwriter*

BEN PATTERSON is the author of *Waiting.* He is a regular contributor to *Leadership Journal* and chaplain of Westmont College.

CHRISTIAN LIVING / PRACTICAL LIFE / GENERAL

ISBN 0-8308-1743-3

9 780830 817436